Watch YOUR Back

How to Avoid the Most Dangerous Moments in Daily Life

Roger Eckstine

Skyhorse Publishing

Skyhorse Publishing books may be purchased in bulk at special discounts for sales promotion, corporate gifts, fund-raising, or educational purposes. Special editions can also be created to specifications. For details, contact the Special Sales Department, Skyhorse Publishing, 307 West 36th Street, 11th Floor, New York, NY 10018 or info@skyhorsepublishing.com.

Skyhorse® and Skyhorse Publishing® are registered trademarks of Skyhorse Publishing, Inc.®, a Delaware corporation.

Visit our website at www.skyhorsepublishing.com.

10 9 8 7 6 5 4 3 2 1

Library of Congress Cataloging-in-Publication Data is available on file.

Cover design by Tom Lau
Cover images courtesy of iStockphoto
Photos by the author unless otherwise noted

Print ISBN: 978-1-5107-0271-4
Ebook ISBN: 978-1-5107-0272-1

Printed in China

Watch YOUR Back

"There is no freedom without safety."
—R. Eckstine

CONTENTS

INTRODUCTION

My father once told me never to remember anything that wasn't important. Somehow I am just not wired that way. It's not that my mind is cluttered with things that aren't important; it's just that I seem to have this innate magnetism that's always looking to make connections between events or nouns (i.e., a person, place, or thing). Sometimes I have to turn things around so the polarities link up like the magnets beneath two little black and white toy dogs we used to play with. It's as if an automatic continuum is the key to my circuit board. So when I tell you that I never intended to write more than one book I am not lying. I am just a victim of my own DNA.

If you are familiar with my first book, *The Shooter's Bible Guide to Knives*, you might recognize it primarily as a review of available knives, knife construction, and a series of overviews of different knife makers. Though unavoidably set in a specific time period, the selection of knives in the catalog section wears extremely well because, as a collection of classic and brand new offerings, they've proven to be timeless. Perhaps that's why sales of the book continue at a steady pace.

Another reason for the continuing success of the *Guide to Knives* might be the one chapter where a risk was taken, unprecedented in the pages of the prolific *Shooter's Bible* series, which goes back more than forty years. Heretofore, the *Shooter's Bible* was primarily a presentation of available arms and accessories, but with little if any instruction put forth regarding how to use them for anything other than sporting purposes. But in the chapter entitled "Folding Knives for Self Defense," we walked a thin line, offering the reader a series of techniques on how to use a common pocket-clip folding knife as a defensive tool. Based on the first day of Brian Hoffner's Defensive Folding Knife Training course, there was one technique in particular that I think sums up a most basic fundamental of personal defense. With the knife unfolded and edge forward, Brian stands his ground while he demonstrates moving the knife continuously in the pattern of a figure-eight in front of his upper body. The result was a whirlpool of blades that Hoffner likens to that of a blender.

The danger is obvious but the key is that it is he (or she) who chooses to advance that asserts them as the aggressor. Presenting this information may have been risky in the context of the *Shooter's Bible* format, but it was probably what led to being offered my next assignment.

The Shooter's Bible Guide to Home Defense offers recommendations for hardening the home structure itself and building a defensive plan based on whatever tactical advantages the interior of your home might offer. There are also options in security systems and technology, learning to recognize the common ploys of home invaders, and preamble to attack as well as legal constraints and how to choose weapons to suit not just your own physical capabilities but also characteristics of the premises as well. With arson being a popular method of revenge, there's also a chapter on fire prevention and survival. But the task of building a game plan for everyday survival covered in *Watch Your Back* was at once more cerebral in nature and inherently more complex.

In the *Guide to Home Defense*, I ask the reader to imagine the view from the front window of the home as a stage and think of themselves as being the director of a high school play. If that sounds hokey, I must

A keystone of Brian Hoffner's Defensive Knife methodology is driving the knife in a continuous figure-eight pattern to protect the head and upper body. What makes this tactic defensive rather than offensive in nature is that it is they who choose to breach this perimeter who assert themselves as the aggressor. In these three images, Hoffner defines the central guard position and the lateral boundaries of the danger zone utilizing the Beast, a knife of his own design.

admit it felt corny even to me while I was writing it. But as the director you would be familiar with every one of the players, what they were supposed to do, and what was going to happen. This was a conceptual aid to make you more aware of how anything that was out of the ordinary could spell trouble, such as a strange car, a door left open, lights left on, etc. When I noted that *Watch Your Back* was going to be a more cerebral study than the *Guide to Home Defense*, and at the same time be more complex, that's because the stage on which threats to survival play out is not only more diverse but also inherently less familiar.

When you are at home it's easy to respond to an unexpected doorbell in the middle of the day by standing away from the front door with body partially shielded by a doorframe. It's your house and "home field advantage" means you've worked out ahead of time just where to stand for cover or concealment, where your chain of improvised weapons and firearms can be found, retreat options, phone access, etc. But outside the home, vulnerability is as unpredictable as the world around you.

Certainly we all feel more comfortable going to the same stores and gas stations based merely on familiarity, and there is an edge in being able to recognize who belongs there and who doesn't. But the added danger is that of a false sense of security. The truth of the matter is we all go places from time to time that we are not familiar with and interact with people we don't know. The fact is, no matter where you go, most of the people you see (and the vast majority of people who see you) are strangers. And if your job is meeting the public, or takes place in public, the erosion of any type of safe distance is exponential.

This book is about the dangers we face inherent to the things we do away from the safety of home field advantage. This could mean as simple a chore as going to the gas station or activities tied inextricably to your job. We'll take a look at what can be done to provide a measure of safety, but I warn you it's not going to be perfect. One proposed title to this book was *How to Avoid a Bad Day*. But any time you are faced with danger, win or lose, it's not going to qualify as what I would call a good day.

Maybe the sum total of my own experiences has turned me from being an idealist to a skeptic. After all, if an obsession with threat analysis is not akin to skepticism, then what is?

Chapter 1 Understanding Preemptive Behavioral Response

Gunfights in the Old West are among the most romanticized of all American lore. But by many accounts most gunfighters did not actually face off, agreeing to such rules as "When the music stops, draw!" Killers often ambushed their rivals by shooting them in the back. Imagine the surprise if one would-be victim was wearing a bulletproof vest, turned around, and shot back? The forethought of strapping on a vest could be referred to as a preemptive behavioral response.

Preemptive behavioral response is very specialized terminology referring to possibly the greatest lesson to be learned in terms of everyday survival skills. The wording might seem confusing because it starts with "pre" yet ends with "response," so let's break it down.

Webster's Dictionary defines preemptive as "designed or having the power to deter or prevent an anticipated situation or occurrence." For example, if our cowboy had known that someone was in town gunning for him, the act of putting on a bulletproof vest before leaving the hotel would qualify as a response to a specific threat. Let's say wherever our cowboy went he suspected there would be outlaws gunning for him. Then, he'd make it a regular practice of wearing the vest, putting it on each morning without thinking of it as any big deal. His behavior would offer safety by design. Consider this. In the 1950s, connecting a seat belt inside an automobile would have been so rare, odd, and out of place that you would have to remind yourself to do it.

In fact the National Highway Traffic Safety Administration reports that in the year 1996 seat belt use was as low as 61% nationwide.[1] But today, drivers and passengers alike have become so used to wearing a seat belt that most people don't even remember putting theirs on. One might better refer to the 1950s application of a seat belt as a practice. Given how habitually we now strap ourselves in, it could be referred to as behavior.

In order to survive not just an anomaly to our peaceful lives, but a possible ongoing threat, we must develop additional habits not unlike wearing a seat belt or locking the front door to our homes before leaving. As such, the question becomes how to reinforce adequate repetition to develop the necessary safety habits. Do we need someone to nag us, or will that just make for rejection of the practices, much like a rebellious child?

For those who recognize the dangers inherent in their professions, the motivation for developing safe habits is easier to accept than for the average person who has never felt threatened before. For the average commuter that works in an office building and doesn't drive around in a yellow cab (which when I was a cab driver I referred to as a "cash register on wheels"), or work in a check cashing store (I like the term "deer feeder" better), internalizing new standard operating procedures to ensure safety may take more convincing.

Hopefully, adding in a step or two such as always parking front end forward and looking around before exiting the car won't be looked upon with same burden as dieting or giving up smoking cigarettes cold turkey.

None of us likes to be inconvenienced, and that's why the perception of additional safety precautions needs to be changed from being a pain in the neck

The vast majority of people alive today wouldn't remember what it was like to ride in an automobile without a seat belt. Even race car drivers were initially suspicious, complaining a seat belt would cause them to be trapped in burning cars. The businessman pictured here doesn't seem to be inconvenienced at all as he works on his laptop and speaks on his cell phone. If we can accept buckling up, which was once considered a nuisance, then it shouldn't be difficult to adapt our daily routine to include measures of personal defense. *Photo courtesy of iStockphoto.*

Where we go is what we are exposed to. Many people who for one reason or another cannot access a proper bank to cash a check may be forced to utilize a commercial check-cashing store. There is nothing wrong with using one. As with a bank, the primary reason one goes to a check-cashing store is to handle money, either on the way in or on the way out. Therefore, a visit to either establishment is likely to make you more vulnerable to crime. When choosing a bank or a commercial check casher, it is important to take into account the surroundings. Utilizing a bank or cash store in proximity to businesses that either sell alcohol or promote other vices, such as a "smoke shop," means you are likely to cross paths with their clientele. And just because a check-cashing store is open twenty-four hours a day doesn't mean you should go there after dark.

and a waste of time to implementation without undue emotion. I'm sure the physical discomfort of wearing a vest every day is something police personnel would like to do without. But remembering to wear it is regularly reinforced by the painful memory of losing a fellow officer.

Beloved race car driver Dale Earnhardt Sr. had the option of wearing a head and neck restraint, but it was not mandatory and he wasn't comfortable wearing it. The HANS (head and neck support) was developed specifically for race car drivers to prevent basilar skull fractures, also a major cause of death in highway accidents.

The HANS device tethers the head to the body by way of a small harness to prevent the head from snapping forward, injuring or breaking the connection between the head and spine. According to the article "Historic Trauma Cases: Dale Earnhardt" by Cynthia Blank Reid, "A basilar skull fracture is any fracture of the skull that originates in or propagates to the base of the skull."[2]

Earnhardt died at the final turn on the last lap of the 2001 Daytona 500 stock car race when his car impacted the wall head on, but the severity of the impact was not immediately obvious even to the other drivers involved in the very same incident. But Earnhardt suffered multiple injuries, including a basilar ring fracture as a result of his head continuing to move forward and striking the steering wheel due to inertial head loading. Months later, the HANS device was deemed mandatory by stock car racing's governing body (NASCAR). As with modern police,

Before World War II, race cars didn't even have seat belts. Today, the head and neck restraint known as the HANS device is the industry standard. Before its use became popular, Dale Earnhardt Sr. was killed in an accident that upon first viewing was not expected to result in a fatality. Given the option of wearing a HANS device, Earnhardt Sr. deemed it too uncomfortable and, like many drivers at that time, lamented that it might make it too difficult to get out of the car if it caught on fire. But a head and neck restraint would have saved his life by not letting the driver's head shift violently beyond its natural tether. Renowned American Sprint Car Series driver Tommy Bryant knows this and wouldn't think of firing up his 800 hp beast without one. Like all modern athletes, Bryant practices safe habits of preparation because doing so affords him the best chance of continuing to enjoy life.

contemporary racers have put aside their objections to proven safety gear and learned to ignore the impulse to complain. For these people, the necessary preemptive behavioral response of gearing up is hardly noticeable because behavior has been transformed into habit.

Not all preemptive behavioral responses are as pointed as putting on a helmet or a bulletproof vest. There are many smaller, more subtle, precautionary actions we can internalize that protect us from harm. For example, several years ago it was pointed out to me that every time I stopped for gas I would start the pump and then proceed to walk around the car. On that particular day, the weather was cold and blustery so why didn't I just get back into the driver's seat and warm up? Asked what I was doing, I blurted out that I was inspecting the tires and checking to see if all the lights were intact. This pronouncement was accompanied by the most incredulous of feelings. It was as if someone had yanked me out of bed in the middle of the night and asked me what I was doing. Doesn't everybody check the condition of the car during a gas stop? I guess you could say this was one preemptive behavioral response I could perform in my sleep.

How did I get to the point where walking around the car during gas stops was habitual to the point of being almost unconscious? Was I copying an elder, or had there been a bad experience when simple inspection would have saved me the trouble of being stopped with a flat tire? Actually, it was both. In my father's time, tires and lights were the least reliable components of automotive construction and I've had my share of blowouts, too. So there was a direct reinforcement of the behavior from which to develop an SOP, or standard operating procedure. My experience told me that someday a simple inspection process would save me from a situation that could be anything from annoying to dangerous. Have you ever tried to change a tire on a busy street or expressway? What if the tire blew out at high speed or some helpful strangers showed up to do me harm? I'd rather walk around the car and troubleshoot no matter how cold it gets.

Many of the preemptive behavioral responses in this book were developed after action, but in the meantime too many people have had to pay too high a price. No one should have to suffer to learn how to set up precautionary measures. We can all learn to engage in "preventive maintenance" that builds in a measure of safety if we are willing to internalize or better yet "habitualize" security measures preemptively. Sometimes this isn't easy, or just too tempting to bypass. The real question becomes, "What does it take for you to willingly accept the performance of precautionary actions throughout your day in order to increase the chances of your survival?"

There's a lot of pop psychology or "psychobabble" out there about behavior and how to enhance or change it. One of my favorites is satisfying or embracing the "inner child." To me the inner child is the immature voice that acts as though there will always be someone or something to fall back on. I hope there will always be a place in your life for the inner child, but it is the voice of responsibility that protects us and it must learn to holler loud and clear.

The problem is most people do not take up methods of personal defense until after something has happened to them or a loved one. Certainly the vision of tragedy or violence is a great motivator. Yet, many people who desire more effective means of personal security find it difficult to implement proven preemptive behavioral responses as a course of action. It's a type of learning disability that has forever fascinated me. Whenever I cannot get myself to learn something, I look for a way to trick myself into doing it. In fact, I thought I was the only one doing this until I read *Practical Shooting, Beyond Fundamentals* by Brian Enos.[3] It seems that Enos and his buddy Rob Leatham were practicing high speed competitive shooting so diligently they would sometimes get stale and stumble trying to perform the simplest draw or reload. To combat this they developed the "Trick of the Day" as a temporary distraction to "quiet the mind." It was something to throw them off just enough so that they'd have to concentrate brick by brick on their technique rather than take any shortcuts and miss out on performing a necessary fundamental along the way.

Out of curiosity, I turned to the world of child psychology to see if there was any way of breaking through to the child that was suddenly being stubborn and didn't want to learn. Consider the study found in the Sage Journals entitled "Using Pre-task Requests to Increase the Probability of Compliance for Students with Severe Disabilities" by George H. S. Singer, Joanne Singer, and Robert H. Horner[4]. The initial description or Abstract refers to the challenge of seeking "a non-aversive procedure to increase the probability that students with moderate and severe handicapping conditions will follow a directive to begin to work." In this case the students, "age 7 to 10 years with documented IQ scores between 20 and 44," have much more to complain about than the average healthy child. And so did their teachers. Bouts of noncompliance included violent behavior toward classmates, including hitting, biting, and scratching. In this test case the request being made of the students was simply to come into the classroom and sit in their designated seats so class could begin. The problem was the students wanted to remain in recess and continue to play in the yard; in technical terms a "transition from play to work."

What the study found was a simple strategy for increasing the probability of a positive response. Instead of jumping right to the endgame command to take their seats, a series of tasks that had the greater likelihood of being completed were requested. Requests such as "give me five," "look at me," or "say my name" resulted in an acceptance of interaction and led to compliance. When this technique was not used students' compliance rapidly diminished. An earlier study by Englemann and Colvin (1983)[5] shared in this conclusion by suggesting that a difficult request should be preceded by rapid series of short, easy requests.

For the soldier in the field that must leave a safer position of cover while bullets are flying by, an inner voice may appear in a moment of doubt. To allay doubt and enable the soldier to continue his mission, this voice would most likely go through a short series of pre-task questions or drills. One such drill would be to concentrate on a breathing pattern commonly referred to as tactical or combat breathing. As detailed in U.S. Army Ranger Lieutenant Colonel David Grossman's book *On Combat: The Psychology and Physiology of Deadly Conflict in War and Peace*, the drill consists of a repetition of breath such as intake through the nose, hold for four seconds, release through the lips to the count of four seconds, and repeat. Sometimes a distraction such as the aforementioned trick of the day can be used to change one's focus from imagining a negative outcome to the mechanics of the job at hand. In one instance, Master Sergeant Paul Howe, proprietor of the Combat Shooting and Tactics school in Nacogdoches, Texas, and a veteran of many battles including Mogadishu (see *Blackhawk Down*), reports running between points of cover using a specific technique whenever there was room to do so. As I understand it, whenever possible, Howe would back off from the edge of cover and get a running start rather than expend the initial moments of exposure trying to pick up speed. Pre-task requests, such as looking for room to build up speed or checking your gear (magazines, check, knife, check...), are easier tasks to fulfill than making it across the field of fire. Paying attention to the details rather than the magnitude of what you are about to do may be all that's needed to propel you into action. For anyone whose job it is to collect from a series of vending machines, one might also develop a Q&A program to invoke a mindset at a higher state of alert. The key is to keep the pre-task requests simple (a few quick, positively answered questions are better than one that requires debate) is the better way to construct a chain of positive thought.

Thinking in terms of pre-task requests and non-aversive procedure may also be helpful in accepting the process of putting extra precautions into action even when the behavior seems unnecessary. In other words, you are adopting preemptive behavioral response as standard operating procedure. For example, putting a dispenser of pepper spray on your belt when you only intend to weed the garden in your own fenced yard may seem unnecessary. For our purposes, the voice in your head saying you won't need the pepper spray could parallel the objections of the students in the Singer study that wanted to stay outside and play.

Objecting to carrying pepper spray when not even leaving the "safety" of one's yard ignores a basic fundamental of preemptive behavioral response. To always carry some sort of defense with you outside or in and around the home is valuable in maintaining the habit no matter how remote a threat may seem. The desired result is that someday you won't even remember taking it with you but it will be there when you need it to fend off an aggressive stray dog. Then again, what is the likelihood of being attacked in one's own yard by a complete stranger after virtually no interaction, inflammatory or otherwise?

Spending the day gardening in her own gated yard, a seventy-nine-year-old Texas woman was murdered in April of 2015 by a deranged man described as being homeless. This same man, later identified as Cavales Prater, thirty-five, attacked his own mother just two days later. In this attack, Prater was interrupted by his mother's roommate and fled the scene. Reportedly, the roommate followed Prater, who was later arrested by police.

No motive for either crime has been established but Prater was described as being seen hanging around local convenience stores and acting unpredictably. County court records showed several arrests dating back to 1998 for convictions of marijuana possession,

theft, and assault on a family member. The fatal attack on the woman, who was a complete stranger to Prater, involved an escalation of violence throughout multiple locations, moving from the garage area to inside a locked bathroom in the house, during which the victim was struck with a golf club, strangled, and stabbed with a scissors. The woman's husband was alerted but was too late to render aid. A homicide detective for the Houston Police Department was quoted as saying, "I believe this to be a random act of violence by a crazy, demented person."[6]

If we could make sense of the perpetrator's actions, would it be more useful to know why the man attacked the woman in her yard or the reason why Prater cut short his attack on his mother two days later? I would say the latter. While it does not seem likely that Prater was overpowered, it was reported that the roommate, who was neither identified nor described in physical detail, was able to pull Prater off of his mother, at which time he fled. Perhaps simple discovery was enough to end the assault. In lieu of the ability or lack thereof for the victim in the fatal attack to defend herself with a lethal weapon, the deployment of any type of weapon immediately accessible might have prolonged the attack, offering a window of opportunity for help to arrive.

Preemptive behavioral response is preparation. In order for it to be effective, it has to be consistent. In order for preparation to be consistent, the actions taken need to be accepted in a manner that does not distract or feel out of place. For example, it's perfectly natural to iron a blouse or shine one's shoes before going to a job interview because it is your desire to improve your life. In terms of personal defense, preemptive behavioral response is perfectly natural because it is the embodiment of your desire to survive. The goal of learning any set of preemptive behavioral response is to internalize it to the point of becoming habit, therefore crossing over into the realm of behavior, or as I like to refer to your collective well of safe habits, your Internal Security Protocol.

Chapter 2 What Everyone Can Learn from the Dangers of Selling Real Estate

Real estate agents face a number of threats because, at one time or another, an agent is going to be alone in a vacant building with a complete stranger or a group of strangers. This is part and parcel of the business and the vulnerability is obvious. Yet the level of threat is dependent on a number of factors. Some are built-in and unavoidable. Others can be controlled. In order to understand the likelihood and prevention of incidents, it is helpful to study how real estate agents attract customers and how the sales process itself is structured.

There are two roles in which a real estate agent can operate. One is that of selling agent and the other is referred to as a listing agent. When acting as a selling agent, he or she represents a customer in search of property to buy. A listing agent specializes in developing an inventory of property for sale. Properties for sale typically appear on the Multiple Listing Service website or MLS. The MLS is an online database that serves as a catalog of available properties complete with specifications, pictures, and general description. The MLS allows the agent to help the customer choose which properties they would like the agent to show them before leaving the office.

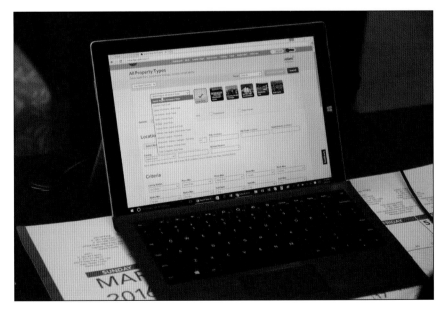

Minimizing the danger of meeting a complete stranger at a vacant house begins with asking the customer to come in to the office to search the Multiple Listing Service (MLS) website. It should be company policy that all first contacts be made at the office and all prospective clients should be properly identified. Not only does this provide a degree of security for sales personnel, searching the MLS based on the buyer's specific needs and priorities is the best way to serve the customer.

Most agents begin their careers as a selling agent waiting in queue at the office for their turn to work with the next customer. While the listing agent seeks to attract customers that already own real property, the selling agent is more likely to work with strangers of unknown means who call on the telephone or walk in off the street. That's why the selling agent is typically more at risk.

Although an agent can in some cases work as both a selling agent and a listing agent (just not on the same deal), most agents prefer to specialize in one role or the other. Those who specialize in being a listing agent tend to be more experienced. One reason is that in order to win the approval of a customer with a home to sell, they should already have a track record of completed or closed sales with which to impress the property owner. Some listing agents concentrate on marketing their inventory to other agents or develop a network of buyers that are looking for rental property. With this strategy, they can avoid working directly with the public at large.

Not everyone gets into real estate sales through working with an established agency. And not every listing agent fits into the system of recognized realtors. People who buy run-down property or properties that have been foreclosed upon are looking to renovate and sell, or "flip," properties for a profit. Either way, this approach can introduce a higher level of risk when compared to listing homes in top condition located in prominent neighborhoods. Homeless squatters may inhabit abandoned properties, making them dangerous to visit. In addition, abandoned properties are difficult to secure from vandalism and loss of investment by arson is another common risk.

Foreclosed, damaged, or abandoned properties are often located in neighborhoods scarred with higher rates of violent crime. When previewing less expensive homes for listing in a seemingly-nice neighborhood,

make sure to look for exterior doors with more than two locks. Check the frames of exterior doors for cracks and obvious damage that would indicate it was previously forced open.

Whether you are a selling agent or a listing agent, you have the choice of where and when you work. Be aware that the location, condition, and the types of homes you show can determine the level of threat you may need to contend with.

Sometimes personality plays a part in whether a person specializes in being a selling agent or a listing agent. No matter how much society changes, women will forever be connected by nature to the home. According to the National Association of Realtors (NAR), there are about two million real estate agents nationwide, including those that operate without membership in the NAR. Fifty-seven percent of these agents are female. Median age is fifty-six years old. Whether it's a homeowner trying to come to terms with the necessity of moving from a place with cherished memories where children were raised, or a newlywed couple looking for their first home, trust in a mother figure can offer the female agent a built-in advantage. Furthermore, the job's flexible hours make real estate sales an ideal job for mothers with children in school or for empty nesters.

In most states it is mandatory for the prospective licensee to be sponsored by a licensed real estate broker. A real estate broker may also be active in sales and it is the brokerage license that provides the legal right to list and sell property. As such, sales agents work under the umbrella of the broker, who is either independent or affiliated with a larger company or franchise operation. Nevertheless, each sales agent must generate their own business. This is where problems, particularly for female agents, can arise.

Perhaps there's been too much influence by television, but the demand for a glamorous appearance

Scarred or repaired doors are red flags indicating the property has been broken into at least once before. What this says about the property and the surrounding area should be of concern to the prospective real estate listing agent as well as to buyers. Be aware that the location, condition, and the types of homes you show can determine the level of threat you may need to contend with. *Photo courtesy of The Door Refinishing Company*.

has become a driving force in advertising. No one can really tell how skillful or how honest a real estate agent will prove to be by looking at a picture on a billboard. This goes for men as well as women. But to the predator, a good-looking woman is the more preferable target. When it comes to advertising, keep in mind you are not the product. Your services are the product. No one is going to say, "What do you mean the deal fell through? You're so pretty." Or, "But you're so handsome and well dressed."

Even if you have already posted pictures of yourself that highlight an attractive or provocative appearance, this doesn't mean you have to follow through with dressing "to the nines" every day. Your work and showing attire should be modest and professional. By modest, I mean attire that is not revealing or suggestive in any way. When asked about the glamorous you that appears on billboards, just say that's the "Hollywood" me. Your showing attire should also be comfortable and, in a sense, athletic. That way, if you have to defend yourself or make a run for it, your clothing will not get in the way or otherwise limit your movement.

Many agents use glamour shots for their business cards but consider taking a cue from headshots used by actors and actresses looking for a movie or television role. If you've ever met a model, TV, or movie star, you'll notice right away that in many cases they do not look quite the same. That's because professional headshots are produced not to show how the person looks in real life but how they will appear on the big screen. Some actors even take headshots geared toward a specific role. Instead of merely trying to look your best, consider having yourself photographed as if you were going to audition for the role of a successful businessperson. According to Deb Wallace, proprietor of Barfield Photography in Houston, Texas, portrait photography can be engineered toward role-play just as certain techniques are employed specific to

wedding photography in order to bring out the purity and beauty of a new bride.

Before presenting a series of incidents in which real estate agents were the victims of crime, let's take a look at what standard operating procedures, indeed preemptive behavioral responses, are already built into the process to protect the agent. In short, what precautionary measures are readily at the real estate agent's disposal.

There are a number of safeguards available to the real estate agent and such protocol is not to be taken lightly. Initial contact should always be face to face. If someone calls in about a property, make any excuse you can think of but get them to come into the office. Offer to show them a preview of the house on the computer first. Tell them about the Multiple Listing Service website, where they can view the interior and find out all the specifications and costs attached to the property. Enthusiastically inform the customer that the MLS will enable them to compare it to others with all the characteristics they are looking for. A good lie like "I'm waiting for another agent to return to the office with the key, why don't you come over in the meantime," should work. Of course, there's always the default "fallback" position of it being company policy for all customers to come into the office first for a "buyer consultation." And this should not be a lie. Offering a buyer consultation is not only a valuable service to a genuine customer but also provides a considerable measure of security. Most perpetrators will not be willing to sit through a meeting describing key points of the buying process such as property search, the closing process, and lender requirements, let alone verification of identity.

In any first contact between sales personnel and a prospective customer, there will be the necessary exchange of pleasantries for the purpose of bonding. From the customer's standpoint, the professional stature of the salesperson is already in place. At the very least, the customer can be sure the sales personnel are who they say they are and their motives revolve around selling or leasing property. The agent, on the other hand, has no idea who has just walked into their office or approached them at an open house. Identifying the customer is the first and most crucial firewall.

Once verbal introductions are out of the way, discussion of what the customer is looking for should offer insight as to whether their goals are realistic. If the customer is unclear, they may just be uninformed as to how a real estate office operates or their motives may not be genuine. The next step a sales agent should take is to qualify the customer's ability to get a loan. If it hasn't been done so already, this is a good time to formally establish identification, beginning with taking a photocopy of their driver's license. This should not raise any objections whatsoever. If the customer shows any hesitance at all, that's a red flag. Either they are not serious customers or they may indeed be dangerous.

Not everyone who shops for a home understands how much money they will actually need. Nor are they always sure they can qualify for a loan. By qualifying the customer's credit status, the agent should be able to find out if they are truly ready to buy and if working with the customer is going to be worthwhile. Of course, not even the ability of the customer to pay for property is a guarantee that a sale will be made. And the claim of being a cash customer should not be a signal for the agent to lower their guard. A good question to ask before agreeing to show property anywhere but on the computer should be, "Is there anything that would prevent you from buying a house today?"

The previous paragraph may well be found in "Real Estate 101." However, the above procedures will not shield the agency from someone with false or stolen identification. Identification theft for the purpose of buying property or obtaining funds under false pretenses in general does not usually take place in face-to-face situations at a real estate agency. The more typical schemes involving real estate and identity theft are found in the arena of ID thieves posing as the owner and obtaining funds via a home equity line of credit for property they do not own. Such schemes can actually be revealed when the real estate agent investigates the credit of a completely honest customer. According to Paul Wylie, founder and former owner of Metrocities Mortgage, in an article published at ProtectMyID .com, an arm of the credit giant Experian, "Too often a victim does not learn of the identity theft until a mortgage originator pulls his credit score in preparation for a home loan."[1]

For any business that makes sales based on the customer's ability to pay on credit or borrow money, rule number one is to identify the customer. Let's take a look at how to spot a phony or questionable ID. While you should be familiar with what your state driver's license looks like, a buyer may be coming from another state and you may not be familiar with what that license should look like. This can be checked by searching that state's website. One preemptive behavioral response would be to visit the Department of Motor Vehicles websites of all bordering states and memorize what the license from each state should look like. In addition, research the licenses from such states that people are most likely to emigrate from. For example, a real estate agent in Florida should be very familiar with a driver's license from the state of New York.

Pay attention to the quality of the license regarding materials and construction. Look for paper that has been laminated or laser printed. New licenses in many states now have the state crest or other insignia embedded by a pattern of holes so holding the license up to the light can be revealing. In addition, there are patterns and holograms unique to each state of issue. The next time you travel by air, be sure to watch how the TSA officer checks your license before entering the gated area. They will hold your license beneath an ultraviolet light in order to view anti-counterfeiting images not visible in common ambient light. You can

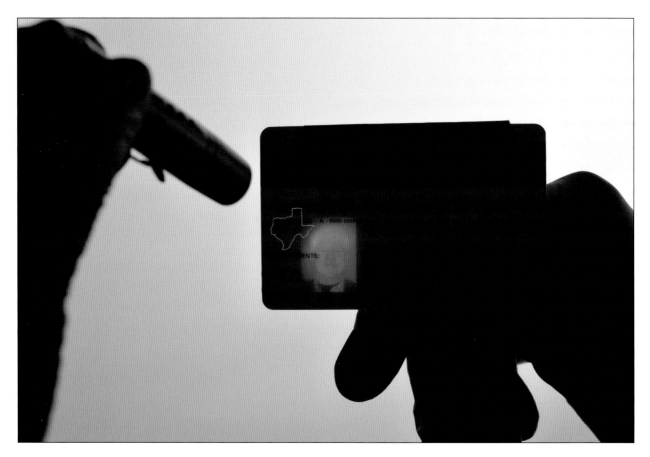

Identifying your client begins with a look at a state-issued ID, most commonly a driver's license. There are many ways a phony driver's license can be reconstructed to appear genuine, but the beam of an ultraviolet flashlight will reveal the truth. An outline of the state of issue may be visible when held up to a common table lamp but a separate holographic image of the rightful owner will show up on the reverse side under ultraviolet light. Small pocket lights like this one from 5.11 Tactical are inexpensive and legal to own.

also benefit from this preemptive behavioral response. Small handheld ultraviolet flashlights are legal to own and should cost no more than twenty to thirty dollars, so it's reasonable to keep one handy.

Whenever you are presented with an out of state driver's license or other ID, the most natural question is to ask why they are moving. It can be presented as little more than small talk so why not probe. Keep in mind that no one is going to come right out and say, "To avoid child support payments" or any other sort of negative admission. Rule 1A when asking questions related to veracity is to follow the most basic of SOPs (standard operating procedures). Take a deep breath,

look them straight in the eye, and ask the question. Trained con artists know how to lie but there really aren't as many "evil geniuses" as you may imagine. If they avoid eye contact while answering, there may be a problem. If they take a deep breath and look you in the eye before answering, they may be one of the evil geniuses in training.

"Is this your current address?" is pretty standard repartee so have some additional questions ready. Follow-up questions can be probing without necessarily being followed by the vocal inflection of a question mark. For example, "I like you better as a blonde" if they are blonde in the picture and the hair color has changed or, "I like contact lenses better than glasses, don't you?" if corrective lenses are specified and there's no evidence as such. Weight can vary but the person's height should be in line with whatever it says on the license. If you're not good at guessing people's height, the average doorway is about 80 inches or 6 feet, 7 inches high. You can memorize or even unobtrusively mark different points on a doorframe. The whole idea is if you are 5 foot 9 inches tall, someone else listed at that height on his or her driver's license shouldn't tower over you.

Just because you are being cautious does not mean you have to be outwardly militant or severe in attitude while communicating with a prospective client about identification. Follow the example of patrolmen who pull over strangers all the time and report that keeping a playful mindset can de-escalate a traffic stop with questions like "You're not carrying anything dangerous are you? No anti-aircraft missiles, tanks, nuclear weapons, or stale cheese?" If the subject starts sweating instead of laughing, you know there's a problem.

One of the quick links or "favorites" a real estate agent has on their computer, iPad, smartphone, or other online device would most assuredly be the local Multiple Listing Service website. In order to be ready to service a client this would qualify as a preemptive behavioral response. So would doing a simple Internet search for the client's name, but here's a better source. Every county or state has a criminal database. All you have to do is enter last name, first name, and date of birth. Have the link for a criminal database ready to go on your Internet device.

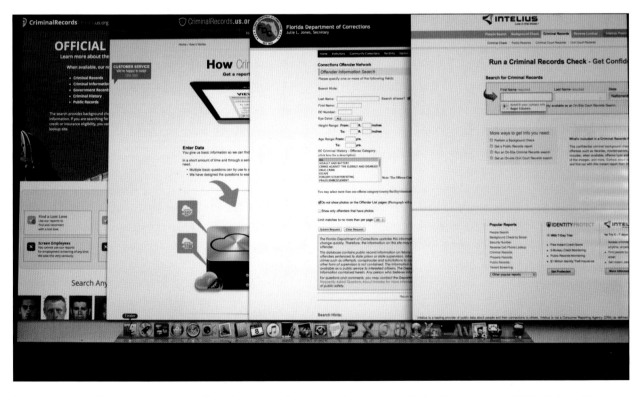

If you have any suspicion about a prospective client, the Internet affords plenty of opportunity to find out just whom you might be dealing with. Even a general search on Google or Bing can be revealing, but why not subscribe to a couple of different services? County clerk and state corrections department websites can also be helpful, but such records are often limited to crimes committed only in the specific county or state. Bear in mind that not all criminal behavior real estate agents are subjected to involves assault. Fraudulent loans and identification theft are other pitfalls of the industry.

Working in sales involves focusing on at least two vital elements, finding what the customer wants or needs in terms of product description, and then providing the motivation for them to take action and make the purchase. Meeting your needs (to make the commission) and meeting the desires of the customer are tied together by available inventory and the salesperson's skill of presentation. Taking into account the customer's needs and your own needs is not exactly like being of two minds. But whenever you are among strangers you should operate in two minds of split objectivity, which is when you consciously and continuously view two sides of every situation. Actually, it is not really possible to objectively view the negative and positive possibilities at the same time. Think of it as a tennis match with skepticism on one side of the net and optimism on the other. There will be times when doubt and faith will go back and forth and other times one side or the other will hold serve. The most dangerous time for the real estate agent is when they forget to play the game.

While internally refereeing and keeping score of your doubts versus positives, you should always be in a yellow mental condition. What does this mean? Many years ago, Colonel Jeff Cooper devised a color-coded system to illustrate relative levels of threat. Red is the highest level during which action is not only called for but the threat is fully active and defense should be underway. Orange is the highest level of readiness without taking action. You could say the high diver is on the board and ready to jump. Yellow is a relaxed state of readiness, with the individual remaining vigilant and judgmental of his or her surroundings. In the white state of mind, awareness is inactive or turned inward focused on one's desires or fantasies, totally ignorant of the surroundings.

A sales agent in the white state of mind is probably more focused on imagining what they will do with the commission than any one pitfall that might ruin the sale or pose a threat to their safety. The lure of smooth talk about a cash sale uncomplicated by bank loans and approvals is just what every real estate agent wants to hear. One pitfall that can lure an agent to operate in the white is when accepting a referral from another agent or a past customer. Remember our tennis game. That's great; the referral has a sale off to a great start. But what if there is not a clear reason as to why the referral is being passed on? When the situation is volleyed to the skeptic's side of the net you should hear, "If the customer was such a great opportunity why wouldn't the agent supplying the referral work it his or herself?" It is possible that the past customer may not really know the person being referred. Hopefully the skeptic in you will be there to slow down the action and not skip any of the steps in the sales process that safeguard via preemptive behavioral response.

Working as a listing agent may be inherently safer than working with customers off the street, but there are conditions that can erode the layers of security ordinarily available to the listing agent. The first shield of defense for the listing agent should be knowledge of whom they are doing business with and where they live. Therefore, any crime they commit is less likely to be assisted by anonymity or by being difficult to locate after the fact. But this does not guarantee your safety, especially if you are a new or inexperienced agent and desperately in need of a commission. The following is a tragic example pulled from interviews of several female real estate agents:

"I personally had a seller of a multimillion-dollar property that I had listed. This seller was a friend of a very close friend so I never thought twice about my safety. He was a single man and asked for me to meet him at his home to review the details of the property, electronics system being sold with the home, etc. All of which is common practice. I was a new agent and wanted to do everything myself. I met him at dinnertime and he had ordered in dinner, which he had told me in advance he would because I was coming from a full day of other appointments. This was our "getting to know you" meeting and because he was such a high dollar client, I believed he required some "wooing" to develop rapport. He served wine. I should have declined, but didn't ever think a glass or two would be an issue over a couple of hours. I don't know what was in the wine. There are hours after that point that I don't remember. When I woke up I was in a very compromised position. I thought it was all my fault. That I had asked for this somehow. I won't go into details but this by far was the worst event of my lifetime to date. I was humiliated and so scared. I never reported anything. My family needed the money at the time so badly that I decided I had to see the sale through. I did go to the doctor and thankfully there were no health ramifications. I never went to his home alone and I never met him from that point going forward that we were not in a public place. Hindsight is always 20/20."

It's very easy to see what made this situation dangerous. You don't really know who you are dealing with. The seller was "a friend of a very close friend," thus breaking the listing agent's first layer of defense. Next, consider the seller and the agent. Given the seller owned a multimillion-dollar property, it is reasonable to believe that he is highly skilled and experienced in business matters, including negotiation and spotting personal weaknesses. The agent was likely a neophyte by comparison. Whether or not the agent's drink was actually doctored, this tactic is nevertheless all too common. Simply make it a rule not to drink with clients. "I don't drink," can be the lie that saves your life.

Another lie you can tell yourself is "I don't need this sale." Of course you do, but practice saying it aloud in front of a mirror. The most difficult thing to do is to change your habits and demeanor. Sometimes, according to behavioral therapists, the only way to change your behavior is to make believe you are the

way you wish to be. Copy the actions of your ideal even if it feels strange and uncomfortable. Sooner or later you will find that you do indeed fit the description of the person you want to be. In this case, confident and successful.

Crimes against real estate agents are primarily carried out by "separation from the herd," a predatory practice commonly found in nature. If we were speaking of animals in nature, separation from the herd would be referred to as acceptable behavior because the predator's place in the food chain is meaningful, sustaining itself while removing weaker, slower, or sick animals from the gene pool. In human society, separation is a tactic of cruelty and evil. Unfortunately, going one on one with customers at a remote location or inside a structure that provides concealment, even if it happens to be situated along a busy street, is inevitable. Yet there are still some safe guards available to the agent within the sales procedure if you choose to use them.

The time, date, and property address of each showing should be recorded with the office you work for. Aside from security, this is a necessity strictly from the business side for multiple reasons. First, so the agent can follow up with the prospective buyer. Also, the agent should let the property owner know how well the property is showing and perhaps offer advice to make the property more sellable. An office with several agents will probably have a rotation, meaning if you're out on a call with one customer, then new calls would require the next agent up. And if one of your other customers calls in during your showing, whoever answers the call should know where to reach you. If you work with only one other agent, let them know where and with whom you are going. If no one in the agency is available, a family member or neighbor should have this information.

Whether you have left word with office personnel, family, or a neighbor, set up a time to check in. They should have a reminder alert for the check-in set on their cell phone (setting a cheap alarm clock works, too). Set the same alarm time on your cell phone as well so you can call in on time. This lets people around you know that you are not completely alone. Follow this same protocol (preemptive behavioral response) even when working in pairs with another agent or companion.

Another option to keep in touch is the locator app on a smartphone. However, this app offers only where the phone is with no clue as to the condition of the owner or if the owner is in control of the phone at the time. It could be helpful to investigators in catching a perpetrator after the fact but offers little in the way of prevention. Bear in mind that operating a touch screen cell phone does take time and a fair amount of dexterity so keep the phone unlocked with tracking and rescue icons readily visible.

Services like the MyForce app from myforce.com go a step further by not only offering location monitoring but also providing a live operator in effect acting as a private 911 service. The MyForce app can reportedly monitor hands free so it does have some possibilities as an effective device. Look for more innovations in the communications industry to make the cell phone a more valuable security tool in the future.

Sales agents that work in pairs are much safer than those that work alone, and not just in terms of preventing violent crime. For example, when showing a home to a couple, the presence of multiple agents makes it more difficult for one of the customers to be left alone in one room or another where they could possibly commit a simple theft, such as opening a drawer and taking jewelry. If there are children in the customer party, two agents have a better chance of monitoring their behavior. This could prevent a child from innocently breaking something, such as knocking over a vase.

The personal property of agents can also be at risk. Whenever the agent is distracted problems can occur, especially when working with more than one customer

at a time. While showing the backyard to one member of the customer party, another customer can be rifling the agent's briefcase, jacket, or purse.

Working in pairs may not always be possible, but there are times when it is, in my opinion, absolutely imperative. An open house is a sales strategy in which a home for sale is open to the public on a walk-in basis.

Anyone may walk into the house during the open house time period. Other than when a lone sales agent leaves the office to meet on site with an unqualified total stranger or group of strangers, the open house is potentially the least secure strategy. An open house can be dangerous not only for the sales agents but for customers in attendance as well.

Why then do agencies continue to host open house events? I interviewed Lance Loken, CEO of the Houston-based Loken Group, to get some answers. "Our job is to get exposure for our listings and have as many people walk through the property as possible," said Loken. "We do a Grand Opening open house the first weekend after the home is on the market." The Loken Group was formed when Lance decided to join his wife Karina in selling real estate after the corporation he was working for downsized its executive staff. Karina began as an individual agent with Keller Williams, and today the Loken Group is one of their most successful teams. But how effective are open house events in selling the property anyway? Probably less than 10 percent of buyers actually purchase the subject property after an open house, according to Loken. "But a lot of the sellers ask for the open houses and we accommodate. It's also a way to provide us with buyer leads." Typically hosted by the listing agent, multiple agents on scene not only increase security but also create additional opportunities for sales and for signing up new buyers.

The Loken Group trains agents to plan their open house events carefully, including adequate lead time, offering plenty of opportunity to plan for

According to Lance Loken, CEO of the Houston, Texas–based Loken Group, many sellers request their homes be featured by holding an open house. This is a good way to get new buyers even if the subject home is not sold as a result. But Loken instructs his agents to get there early so they can greet customers with less distraction and to work in pairs for greater security.

An electric sign-in pad offers security options not available to a paper and pen. Connected to Wi-Fi, the same pad can be used to quickly access background-check search engines while on site.

security. "Get there early so you aren't in a rush and distracted when people start coming through the door," offers Karina Loken. Other tips include using doorstop alarms for secondary exterior doors in order to monitor how many people are present and where they are situated, as well as to afford warning of an attack.

You should also make sure that the seller has stored and secured all valuables. Jewelry is what typically comes to mind, but additional items not usually thought of as valuables include prescription drugs and personal mail, which can lead to identity theft. And don't be afraid to ask the homeowner to lock up weapons and firearms.

If the attending agents are licensed to carry a concealed firearm, encourage them to keep them at hand and under their control; the firearm should be holstered on their person or inside a day planner designed for concealed carry. The Hidden Agenda from Galco Gunleather also functions as a day planner that can be used for taking notes on the comments of prospective buyers as they tour the house.

Even more handy is Galco's iDEFENSE. The iDefense folio carries not only a defensive handgun, but also accommodates a tablet computer.

Holstered carry is superior to alternate methods of carrying a firearm because there is far less chance of leaving the gun where it can be discovered, lost, or

The doorstop alarm is a simple and inexpensive device that sounds an alarm as the door opens and hits the pressure plate. Not only is this a good travel companion for hotel room doors, but it can also offer added security during an open house by limiting access to only the front and rear doors.

It's difficult to argue with the versatility of a writing pad complete with calendar, especially when it zips up in a leather case with lanyard so you won't easily forget to take it with you. It's even better when it offers the facility to carry a handgun with spare magazine. The Galco Hidden Agenda fills multiple roles, shown here with a 9mm Smith & Wesson M&P Shield. The initials M&P stands for Military and Police but the Shield has nevertheless become one of the most popular civilian handguns of all time.

A key part of setting up an open house is to create a station where potential buyers sign up and take one of your business cards. But once your setup is complete, be sure to stow your briefcase, bag, or personal items out of sight. Distracted by working with multiple customers with no way of knowing if they've signed in with an alias or if they've signed in at all, this realtor's bag is at risk.

If a client on scene needs more information or would like to see additional properties, the portability of an iPad, shown here in a Galco iDefense planner, means you won't have to go back to the office to look on a computer. This also offers the ability to perform background checks on the go.

The Galco iDefense planner not only protects your computer but can also help you protect yourself and others. The iDefense provides a secure holster for carrying small to medium handguns and a pouch for a spare magazine or speed loader. The Smith & Wesson model 340 PD is capable of firing .38 Special or .357 Magnum ammunition so it's plenty rugged. Weighing in at only about 11 ounces, you'll hardly notice the additional weight.

stolen. It's not a secret that real estate agents take pride in their appearance and whether the gun is carried concealed or openly, the variety of upscale and exotic holster and belt combinations currently available are more expensive but not difficult to find.

The primary vulnerability inherent to the selling agent is that they must leave the office to show multiple properties. In doing so, not only are they leaving the relative safety of the office and the presence of additional personnel, they will also be driving in their personal car. Since an automobile is a likely necessity for the real estate agent, the cost of the car is at least partially tax-deductible. Most agents find it necessary to have a nice car whether they actually transport customers or not, making them a target for auto theft.

The problem of auto theft for real estate agents exists on two levels. On one level, vulnerability to auto theft is no greater than for anyone else. Cars can be secured with ignition shutoff features, auto tracking devices,

and, of course, audible alarms. Where the car is parked can make it less vulnerable, and making sure it is locked without any valuables visible from the outside also contributes to security. Stopping by the curb and exiting for a moment just to make sure the "For Sale" sign is properly in the ground while leaving the engine running or the driver's side door open could invite a crime of opportunity. When parked and locked, cars can take care of themselves to one degree or another, but you've got to have that inner voice nagging you not to get careless.

If you are familiar with my *Shooter's Bible Guide to Home Defense*, then you've learned that home invasion robberies require the homeowner to be present, otherwise hidden valuables take too long to find. Safecracking is a lost art mostly because it's much easier to convince the homeowner to simply give up the hiding places or provide the combination to a safe. The same goes for carjacking versus common auto theft. Carjacking, like the home invasion, requires the

The dress code for selling real estate is typically higher than in other fields, but concealed carry can be classy, too. The exotics line from Galco Gunleather includes a matching ensemble of alligator skin that is just as durable and efficient as any other type of tactical gear.

driver to be in the car. The advantage to the thief is that the car is less likely to be damaged—no broken windows or damaged ignition lock.

Would a car thief go through the process of meeting formally, including registration with a real estate agent, just to steal their car? Probably not, and it seems just as unlikely that two people would team up for such a robbery, one as the client to put you off guard and the other as the thief. But it wouldn't be difficult to stake out an agency and pull off a carjacking just as the agent was getting into their car or arriving at the office. The bigger problem is that there is a moment in almost every carjacking when the decision is made to either abduct the driver and passengers or just take the automobile.

If you have been abducted and your telephone rings with your buddy expecting a status report, you may or may not have the chance to explain to the abductor that if you don't answer, the caller will track your car and/or your phone. Or if your reminder alarm on your phone goes off you may be able to convince them that you have to call in. In either case, any time you are allowed to communicate during your abduction, hopefully it will be with someone that has been prepared to understand sub-messaging or a prearranged code. Everyone in your family as well as the people you work with should be familiar and listening for distress codes. There may not be time or opportunity to interject a color code reference (red for extreme danger) or a sentence that hides an acronym that spells H-E-L-P, but referring to the person on the other end of the phone by the wrong name should set off alarms. And indeed, every car should be set up with a tracking feature.

What Case Studies Tell Us

If there is any doubt about the vulnerability of real estate agents and how ignoring standard operating procedures increase the likelihood of being a victim, the discussion of the following should put them to rest. Neither I nor anyone else should ever say that any plan to avoid harm is foolproof nor is it a guarantee, but consistent use of preemptive behavioral response is the best insulation against crime.

Proper and accurate identification of the customer is probably the biggest weapon in the arsenal for anyone dealing with strangers. According to a January 12, 2015, report on the *Housing Wire* website, an Elk Grove, California, real estate agent was lured to a model home for sale in a new development on a simple show request that came in by telephone. Had the agent properly identified the customer, she would have found out that the caller was David Burnhardt, who authorities later confirmed was a registered sex offender.

When Burnhardt arrived at the model home, he threatened the female agent with a gun and held her against her will. The woman, whose name was not released, was taken to the bedroom and handcuffed. It was reported that he later moved her to a second location inside the residence, continuing to threaten her repeatedly. In a seemingly hopeless situation, luck appeared in the form of precautions taken by the management of the development. Security officers hired to protect the properties from vandalism and other forms of mayhem came into view outside the property. Fearing discovery, Burnhardt removed the handcuffs, told the victim to not draw the attention of the security guards, and ordered her to walk with him to the front door. Perhaps he thought he could drive off with her to another location. In a stroke of either good luck or sound tactics, the woman was able to position herself so that the perpetrator went out the door first. As soon he stepped outside, the woman closed the door and locked it. Unable to get back into the home, Burnhardt chose to escape in his pickup truck parked outside.

After Burnhardt had left, the agent went outside and flagged down a security officer. It was reported that "the security officer, fearing for his safety and the safety of the victim, drove to a nearby shopping area and contacted local police."[2]

Given what happened, it is reasonable to believe that the security officers themselves were not armed, but they did act effectively to the best of their abilities. Aside from the abduction and related criminal behavior, Burnardt stole personal property from the vehicle of the agent, including two cell phones. From further information it is reasonable to believe that tracing of calls made on one or both cell phones were key to his arrest some time later in Modesto, California. At the time of his arrest Burnhardt was found to be in possession of the weapon used in the attack. This was a crime made possible by the lack of pre-identification and meeting alone on scene resulting in what could be viewed as the supply of a victim upon demand.

But not all the risk is in the hands of the selling agent waiting for a call. Agents that buy and sell property sometimes end up with property that will not sell. In order to cut losses, one common avenue to recoup funds is to offer the property for lease rather than let it sit unoccupied, vulnerable to criminal trespass, arson, or vandalism. Liability regarding the likelihood of vacant property being damaged through criminal acts depends largely on location. Some neighborhoods are more dangerous than others and where the agent chooses to deal in property is their choice. But so is how you deal with the administration of each property.

In October of 2008, it was reported that an argument between a real estate agent and her tenant resulted in murder. The slaying occurred during a discussion between thirty-nine-year-old Ricky Powell and seventy-year-old Herta Bailey because Powell had failed to pay his rent. Bailey was choked to death and placed in the trunk of her car. Powell subsequently stole Bailey's credit cards and used them to pay utility bills.[3] We have no way of knowing how Powell came to be Miss Bailey's tenant or how much she knew about his past history.

Whenever a customer buys property for the purpose of leasing, it is common practice for the agent to advise the new landlord to hire a management company. Providing the name of a management company that has been thoroughly vetted is an extra service adding to the value of your practice. In addition, any real estate agent thinking of entering into the field of leasing themselves should also heed this advice. The management company not only services the needs of the tenant regarding repairs, but also collects the rent. As such, the management company works through protocol designed to reduce problems such as evictions and non-payment of rent. The local sheriff or constabulary may also be tasked with security for eviction procedures. In short, it is usually best to enlist an intermediary to handle tenancy.

Let's continue with a study of one of the most widely publicized murder cases of the twenty-first century. On September 26, 2014, forty-nine-year-old Beverly Carter, a sales agent in Little Rock, Arkansas, disappeared after arranging to meet a customer for a series of three showings of homes for sale in nearby Scott, Arkansas. Her body was found days later in a shallow grave on the grounds of a concrete company in Pulaski County. How could this have happened?

In every crime there is motive and opportunity. In a case where the victim and the perpetrator had no prior relationship or dealings, there is no reasonable way in which Mrs. Carter could have contributed to motive such as revenge. Even if she had contributed to motive, the key would have been to limit opportunity or eliminate it completely.

Arron Lewis, age thirty-three, was charged with the crime. Although he pled not guilty, there seemed to be an admission of guilt when Lewis spoke into the microphone of a television reporter in video later supplied to YouTube.com by the *Global Sun Times*. "Why Beverly? Why Beverly?" asks the newswoman as Lewis is being led to transport in a Pulaski County Sheriff patrol car. Lewis, with a subdued look on his face, answers, "She was a rich broker." This would indicate the motivation was money. Indeed, Lewis's estranged wife, Crystal Lowery, was also arrested. It was reported

that the two had argued often when they lived together and that the estranged husband was not able to pay child support. Lowery and Lewis were charged with kidnapping for ransom. But it was Lewis's second response during the broadcast as news cameras and microphones followed him into the patrol car that speaks directly to opportunity. Hounded by the reporter for more answers as to motivation, he spoke again just as the car door was closing. The reporter asked again, "Why Beverly?" Lewis answers almost matter-of-factly, "Because she was a woman who worked alone."[4]

As for Mrs. Carter being "a rich broker," Lewis was wrong about her income. Nor was she a broker at all. Real estate agents are often looked upon as being wealthy simply because they dress nicely and deal with big ticket items, but only a small percentage of real estate agents make a king's ransom. Perhaps the aforementioned trend of some agents presenting themselves like stars adds to the rich "Hollywood" image. But just like many actors and recording artists have learned, fame is not to be confused with fortune.

Lewis was also wrong about her being "a woman who worked alone." She was not alone at the office when the call came in. For insight into how Beverly was "separated from the herd," here are portions of a transcript of an interview aired on the Fox News Channel with her employer and friend Brenda Rhoads, managing broker of Crye-Leike Real Estate in Little Rock, Arkansas. The title of the interview segment was "Raising Red Flags, Realtors Taking Extra Precautions." The host is Steve Doocy.

According to Rhoads, Beverly Carter had the intention of showing three homes to Arron Lewis and then going home for the evening. Miss Rhoads reports this "wasn't anything abnormal."

Doocy: How often do you get calls, "Hey I'm in front of this house at . . . could you come meet me? I'd like to take a look at it." Total stranger, it's going to be an empty house, you're completely vulnerable.

Rhoads: We get those calls I would say on an average of five to ten a day.

Doocy: Because you work largely on commission, it's one of those things if you don't go you don't make money.

Rhoads: We work only on commission. That's the only way we make our money.[5]

On the "Find Beverly Carter" Facebook page, respondents posted advice such as "do NOT go to an appointment alone or even unarmed." Bear in mind this is an assumption that weaponry alone makes you safer or invulnerable.

Aside from recommendations such as safety apps or even firearms, Doocy suggests upon first contact, "If it's a first time meeting, 'Hey meet me over at the headquarters of the real estate office.' What else?" he asks Rhoads.

Rhoads: "That's the most important. They've got to come to the office. We have to see them face-to-face. And the public has to realize that's what's going to happen. It's not going to be that they can just call us and [we] run over at the drop of a hat. They have to realize the safety issues for them as well as us in a vacant house."[6]

So much is revealed by the interview above. When the call for a showing came in, it was as good as anonymous. Based on the perpetrator's own statement of opportunity, he might as well have been ordering a pizza as requesting the presence of "a woman working alone." That the caller was not required to come to the office first was ideal for his purposes. Had Arron Lewis visited the office, he may not have been judged undesirable based on his looks, the way he dressed, or even his demeanor. But when properly identified, a quick search of the criminal database would have revealed no less than four previous convictions on felony charges and he was currently on parole.

In the wake of Carter's death, hundreds of real estate professionals signed a pledge to change how they operate in an effort to ensure their safety. It reads:

I pledge to . . .

Under no circumstances show a home to a stranger without first meeting them at the office or asking them to submit identification.

Educate my clients that open houses are a safety concern both for the homeowner and myself.

Limit open houses as a marketing strategy and/or make prudent and safe decisions about my open house marketing efforts.

Follow my intuition, and not step into situations that I feel uneasy about.

Use the buddy system whenever I am unsure or uneasy about a showing or meeting.

Make myself available to my fellow agents as a "showing-buddy" should they ever feel the need to take someone along or feel unsafe.

Seriously consider the nature of my personal marketing, and its potential impact on my safety.[7]

The pledge was a good start, but with real estate sales being much more complicated than any other type of service, let's see if we can create a more detailed step-by-step procedure that would offer a stronger preemptive behavioral response.

The best place for first customer contact is always at the office. If someone calls in on a specific property, ask if they are already working with an agent. If so, then tell them to have their agent call in to arrange a showing. If not, then have them come in to the office and ask them to sign on with your agency. This presents the lowest risk not just to your personal safety but it greatly increases the opportunity for you to make a sale.

Informal introductions should be followed by formal identification. Be familiar with the proper appearance and construction of state's driver's licenses.

The customer's description of what they are looking for and/or why they are moving should make sense. Serious buyers will already be pre-qualified for a loan or agree to the pre-qualification process. Cash buyers should also be required to offer documentation. Keep in mind the option of referencing the criminal database.

Professional or practiced liars can be difficult to spot, so it wouldn't hurt to be aware of what are considered to be common physical signs someone is lying. Eyes widening, looking away while answering, adding too much detail, or speaking endlessly to wear down the listener are on the list of what to look out for. Gut feeling on your part should never be ignored.

Once the agreement is made to show property, ride in your car so it can be traced.

Better yet, ride in separate cars. If your cell phone requires a code to access the keypad/touch screen, expand the amount of time it takes for it to default to locking out or turn off the lock completely and keep the screen active for immediate access to the telephone. Check for cellular service at each location you visit. Emergency 911 should be on speed dial and entered as AAAAA911 into your personal contacts list so it will appear at the top of page one.

When pulling up to the property, slow down and inspect visually from inside your car before parking. Ask yourself, is someone home? Are any doors ajar, windows damaged, gates open, or is the garage door open? Is anyone waiting nearby in a parked car (especially with the motor running) or standing around in the general vicinity for no visible reason? Do not park in the driveway as your escape is then easily blocked.

After unlocking the front door of the property, tell the customer that you're going in first to make sure no one is home. This gives you the opportunity to lock the door behind you if you feel threatened. Naturally, you could ask the customers to walk past you and enter first but you will probably have your back to them as you unlock the door, giving them the advantage of being able to push you inside. Another tactic is to suggest they walk the exterior of the property to keep them away from you as you unlock the door.

Once inside, positioning becomes all the more important. If at all possible, don't let the customers get between you and the door leading out. Utilize the principle of tethering. A tether is a lead wire cable or rope that connects a moving object to a stationary point. Think of yourself as the stake in the ground. Let the customer move outward via an imaginary tether. Avoid going into attics and basements. Walk behind the customer. Do not enter a room from which there is no escape. As the customers fan out to inspect the room hover by the door or at the top of the stairs. Remember, at any time you can make up an excuse to leave.

You might be wondering if you should even be showing property if you are so concened about your safety. Certainly anyone you deem suspect should have been vetted using the criminal database during the identification process. The purpose of the information above is twofold. One reason is to keep the skeptic—you—in the game. But primarily you will need to develop particular habits of direction and choreography. The customers should be directed or distracted so that they are not directly behind you as you open the door, and once inside they should never be between you and an exit.

When listing a property for sale, make sure that it is located in an area in which you would feel comfortable and safe showing. Think of yourself as the buyer and take a moment to share in the possible liabilities. If it is in need of renovation and the intention is to list it for the owner "as is," make sure the structure is safe to enter and secure from squatters, arson, or vandalism.

When showing a room with only one way out and one way in, always let your buyers enter the room first and watch them from the door as they inspect the interior space. As they fan out stay "tethered" to the entrance/exit. This agent could have shown the garage with the main door open. But walking in via a side door ahead of her clients means she is trapped. This first defensive position shows the agent accessing a weapon hidden inside her purse. Notice her body position. Turned sideways towards whomever she is confronting with elbow in front of her, she is prepared to meet oncoming force. Furthermore, access to the compartment in her purse is shielded in her favor.

The draw is completed with the purse being pulled from over the handgun to a guard position, almost as if it were a shield. The handgun has actually been moved very little to the rear. Keeping the gun close to the body makes it more difficult for an aggressor to grab for it. When fighting at close distances, the gun can actually be fired without being completely raised so long as the shooter's opposite hand is not in front of the muzzle.

With the gun up, the arm and purse may still act as a shield to protect the gun. But it may also be helpful to move laterally. In this case, circling to her right would offer the most speed and stability. Even a small change in position can add distance to the path of anyone who might be advancing and afford additional time for you to respond, not to mention if they have a weapon, a moving target is more difficult to hit.

If you yourself are in fact looking to buy the property and intend to fix it and sell it, get at least three estimates from recommended contractors to make sure the combined cost of purchase and renovation will leave room for profit. You never want to be put in the position of desperation to make a sale tempting you to overlook standard precautions.

Preemptive Behavioral Response for the Real Estate Agent

Checklist

When visiting a property for evaluation, look out for signs that exterior doors have been forced open. Broken trim or an excessive amount of locks may indicate it is located in a high crime neighborhood.

Vacated or abandoned property can be prone to squatters. Check exterior first for signs of break in or trespassing. Be wary of excessive littering inside the property.

Project a businesslike rather than glamorous profile in all forms of advertising.

Wear clothing that is professional but comfortable to provide ease of movement.

Never confuse attracting a customer with wooing a suitor.

All first points of first contact should be at the office. (In the event of an open house agents should be teamed rather than alone.)

Always positively identify the customer before showing property away from the office.

Always pre-qualify the customer's ability to pay cash or obtain financing.

Be familiar with the proper appearance and format of in-state and out-of-state means of identification such as a driver's license.

Don't be afraid to access the state's criminal database when identifying a customer.

Remain in a state of vigilance not just to cues regarding the sales process but also to your personal safety.

For all your wishes to help people make their dreams of owning a home come true, remember the game must also be balanced by your needs to make a profit and to do so in safe environment. Don't worry about putting off customers with procedures in place to ensure your safety. Those with honest intent to buy or sell will always welcome the institution of proper methodology.

When showing, do not enter closets, basements, or dark rooms.

Do not let customers get between yourself and an exit. Tether yourself at the entrance/exit while customers walk inside.

Beware of referrals. Treat referral customers the same way you would any other stranger.

Do not drink alcohol or smoke marijuana with customers.

No matter how much you need the next commission, leaving yourself open to being taken advantage of will not you help make the sale. Remain professional and stick to the proper guidelines.

Always leave word of where you will be showing and with whom to a co-worker or family member. Schedule a time to check in and stick to it.

Maintain an "app" on your phone indicating location.

Install a locating device in your automobile.

Work in pairs whenever possible.

Learn to carry weapons appropriate to whatever laws are in effect in your municipality or state. Make sure you know how to conceal, deploy, and operate such weapons.

If you must approach a leasing customer about late payment, do not do so alone. This goes for male as well as female agents. Keep in mind that you may have the option to request an escort from local law enforcement.

Do not show property after dark.

Don't be afraid to make up an excuse to leave or cancel an appointment.

Keep in mind the most important rule—if you think something is wrong, there is something wrong.

Chapter 3 Fuel Stops—The Great Equalizer

People who live at the base of a volcano are often criticized for living dangerously. So are people who live in parts of the United States where tornadoes rip across the landscape year after year or nearby to rivers and bayous that repeatedly flood. Why don't they just move on? The same goes for people who work at dangerous jobs. Sometimes the critique is at its heart caring yet unavoidably sharp. Other times the criticism is shortsighted, unmasking the speaker as selfish and mean. But there is one risk that nearly everyone across the nation—retired, student, or employed—takes on a regular basis without the least bit of concern. It has little to do with how much money we make or what we do to earn it. It may well be America's most democratic threat. Everybody plays this game but we hardly notice the danger. The game is called "Gas Station."

Before anyone thinks this is a pitch for electronic automobiles, let me say that I find being electrocuted just as scary as burning up. It's just that years ago a trip

Stopping for fuel or service used to mean putting your car in the hands of a professional. Uniformed gas station attendants were not only more adept at operating the pumps but also better able to spot potential problems such as a worn tire or leaking radiator. Coincidentally, the presence of a full-service attendant also provided a potential security guard. *Photo courtesy of iStockphoto.*

to the gasoline station was in many ways much safer. After all, even the least polished gas station attendants were far more practiced than the average person when it comes to filling the gas tank.

Technology has made the pumps themselves safer to use but from the standpoint of security from assault, kidnapping, and theft, the presence of a full service attendant also provided a potential security guard. Today, few gas stations are attached to a garage and the only attendant available is inside a convenience store or bulletproof booth. Now that all services available at the pump are self-service, personal security is your responsibility as well.

Some people say if we just paid cash for our fuel there would be less crime at the pump. They argue the complexity of setting into motion a purchase by credit or debit card is time-consuming and distracting. But whenever the cost of gasoline is high, I should think the necessary wad of cash would offer quite the magnet. And seeing how most people now pay for fuel with a credit or debit card, the vehicle itself is the more likely target of theft even when you consider that pirate card readers and mini cameras threaten the integrity of your account.

Theft of credit or debit card information at the gas pump is becoming more widespread because it is just so easy to do. The most common method is by the temporary installation of a skimmer. The skimmer fits into the slot so that when the card is scanned for payment at the pump it is also stored by the skimmer. The skim-

Card readers with shields made from plastic are my least favorite because the facade can be purchased on the web as a spare part and modified to house a pirate reader, and then placed over the legitimate slot. *Photo courtesy of iStockphoto.*

Whether the reader is designed to access information with the magnetic strip facing upwards or down, what you need to look for is a tight fit for your card without any trace of enlargement. If the slit appears to have been expanded (usually to one side) a miniaturized reader may have been temporarily installed to steal data directly from your card. *Photo courtesy of iStockphoto.*

mer stores the information without interfering with the point of sale. That's why many transactions can take place without the buyer knowing the information was stolen. Once the thief removes the skimmer, the stolen data is used for either online purchases or to create a counterfeit card.

Bluetooth technology has added another dimension to skimming, allowing for information to be downloaded wirelessly. This means it's not necessary for the thief to physically remove the skimmer. Instead, they brazenly download the information they need over the air and leave the skimmer.

Until the charges from the online purchase or the counterfeit card appear on your statement, the victim may remain none the wiser. That's why it's important to check your accounts on a regular basis well before the bill comes in the mail.

The newest credit and debit cards include an icon that contains a radio frequency identification or RFID

"chip." However, this type of card can still be pirated if the card reader is not equipped with RFID technology. In fact, not all machines have, at the time of this writing, been updated to make use of the chip. The more common method of stealing data from cards with RFID technology is for the thief to use a scanner while getting as physically close as possible to the card even when it is inside a wallet or purse, literally pickpocketing the information electronically. Bear in mind that actual contact between the scanner and the card is not necessary.

Use of a debit card at a gasoline station is really a very bad idea. Given we're all walking around with telephones that are also movie cameras it is possible to play back the "film" and copy the personal identification or PIN number. The more likely method of recording the PIN number is by use of a very small camera mounted facing the keyboard or on the buttonhole of a passerby. Combined with information from a skimmer, your account is at risk.

Thankfully, bank issued debit cards can also be used as a credit card. When the option "debit or credit" comes up on the screen, choose credit.

There are a few ways to avoid theft of data at a gasoline station or anywhere else you may use a credit card. If your card is RFID-equipped, purchase a shielded wallet. Unlike the necessity of using lead to shield Superman from Kryptonite, the shield is constructed of a lightweight alloy so you may not even notice the extra weight in your pocket. Another solution, according to Internet chatter, is to wrap your card in aluminum foil, but this does not sound foolproof to me. What if the foil slips off and no longer protects the chip? Keep in mind that there is no good reason why someone should approach you while at the pump and anyone passing by could be trying to scan your card. In fact, not allowing strangers to get close to you should always be a part of your general security.

To avoid the presence of a skimming device, check the pump for tampering. If the face of the pump, especially around the card reader, appears to be damaged, it could mean the casing was removed and a skimmer was installed. The damage need not be severe. Small dents or scratches, or any sign of prying along the seams are meaningful signs. The reader area may also be marked with a security seal placed there by the collection agency. Make sure the seal is only one layer thick. Thieves have been known to cover a broken seal or a void sticker with a counterfeit sticker of their own proclaiming the mechanism is secure.

The only way to ensure that your credit or debit card will not be compromised is to pay by cash. When it comes to robbery, cash is king but not necessarily at the pump. Pay at the pump does not accept cash as it would a credit or debit card. In order to pay cash you must go to the pay window or inside the store. Thieves can tell if someone is likely to make a cash purchase when the driver parks their car at the pump, gets out, and walks towards the cashier. In order to complete this plan, a thief must have at least two essential components in place—some means of intimidation and a getaway plan. Of course, if you are flashing a large sum of money on your way to the pay window, the attraction might spontaneously set into motion a crime of opportunity. A quick mugging can take anyone by surprise. The safest way to fill up via cash is to approach the cashier as inconspicuously as possible and pass them the money. Once the money has been collected, the immediate threat is reduced.

If you are not paying with cash then the focus of the threat will more likely be theft of the automobile itself or its contents. Doors are typically unlocked or left open during a fuel stop and anything left on the seats is subject to a quick grab. Yet, a major obstacle to your security are the sheer variety and number of distractions that come from the credit card process and operating the pump. The challenge is how to remain vigilant while performing all the necessary functions. So let's back up a bit and see if we can choreograph a secure fuel stop with a credit card using a video camera.

As described in Chapter 2, there are four levels of awareness corresponding to a color-coded system beginning with white. White is the state of mind wherein the person is least aware of their surroundings. Someone in the white may see people or objects that are out of place but make no conscious judgment as to the meaning behind them and therefore draw no conclusion regarding how they could affect their safety.

We began our development of a safer gasoline stop with a study of how someone in white state of mind, displaying no conscious effort to ensure his or her own safety, performs a gasoline stop. In the white state of awareness, the driver enters the gas station area and pulls up immediately to the first available pump, turns off the ignition, opens the car door, and moves towards the pump while reaching into the back pocket for his wallet. After fishing for the credit card, he removes it

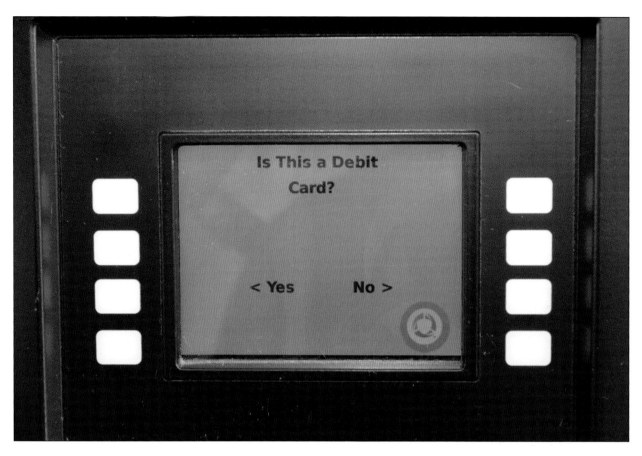

Pay at the pump can require as many as six different steps, including being asked if you have a rewards card, if you want your car washed, or would like to add a fuel conditioner. The one answer you should always give is selecting credit, not debit. It is not uncommon for thieves to use a cell phone to capture one's PIN number on video. Combined with a physical pickpocketing, electronic pickpocketing of the RFID chip, or information gathered from a credit card skimmer installed in the reader slot, your account can be violated.

and adjusts its position so the electronic stripe matches the schematic on the reader. The card is then inserted and pulled out. The first question on the touch screen is "Debit or Credit?" Then, "Use keypad to register zip code and press enter. Do you want a car wash? Yes or no. Do you want a receipt? Choose grade of gasoline and push button. Or, would you like to purchase injection of fuel additive [as if they can prove the chemical is actually being delivered]?"

Some pumps actually begin with an on-screen question of "Are you a member?" for those who have a rewards card that gives a discount for each dollar spent at the pump or at the supermarket the station

is affiliated with. Not only does this extra question add time to the transaction, the card reader may not respond if you ignore it and insert your credit card first. You might not realize why the reader is not responding until you have swiped your card a couple of times. Furthermore, the answers to each question appearing on the screen may need to be answered on the adjoining push buttons and not directly on the screen. Just because there are arrows or other visual calibrations next to each question on the screen, it doesn't always mean it actually functions as a touch screen. Add to this the sensitivity and condition of the buttons or the touch screen and distractions mount up, not to mention frustrations. The next step is to actually handle the pump.

In reviewing a white state of mind fuel stop on videotape, one aspect became immediately apparent. We never saw the face or even the front side of the person getting gas until it they were done with the payment process. Until then the buyer stood with head down totally engrossed in the command screen, completely unaware of his surroundings. It was as if the buyer was in his own visual cocoon.

His attention was completely focused within the small space bordered by the driver's side door, the pump, and the pay screen. The problem was, if we could see the customer's lack of attention on the video, so could anyone else that might be watching. Now, let's compare the fuel stop in white mindset with a stop performed at the same gasoline station but with the buyer in a vigilant yellow state of awareness.

The driver enters the fuel station and drives completely around the station before choosing the pump he wants to use and then drives alongside it. The car stops but the driver does not immediately exit. Instead the driver can be seen checking his rearview mirror and his side

This gentleman is completely consumed by the task of answering questions from the card reader. He should be pacing his actions, looking around to his left and right after answering each question posed by the machine.

mirrors left and right almost as if he were on the high-way preparing to change lanes. He then begins to exit the car. With the door open, he stands and looks left and right before moving away from beside the driver's seat. The open door is still between his body and the pump, blocking anyone that might approach from the front of the car. Looking side to side, he closes the door while simultaneously pulling the wallet from his back pocket. He does not look down at his wallet until it is open and his fingers are indexed above the row of credit card slots.

A quick look down confirms his choice of credit card and once he finds the card reader slot he looks slightly to his right before setting the card into the reader. With card swiped, he wastes no time return-ing it to his wallet, and after checking visually left and right puts his wallet back in his pocket. His head appears to be on a swivel as he brings his hand up to the screen and for each question appears to look left and right.

The buyer in the white state of mind showed no visual field of concentration beyond the line drawn between the pump and the filler cap. The driver in the yellow state of mind continued to punctuate his routine with surveillance, breaking down the procedure into smaller individual chores such as removing the filler handle, head on a swivel, placing the handle into the filler hole, and looking left and right while setting the release.

What to do while the car is being filled with fuel is certainly a valid question. Sitting inside the car allows for you to lock the doors. While this does offer a level of protection from nuisances such as panhandlers or window washers, it also means that in the event of a carjacking you may be trapped inside and unable to escape. And it is unclear if the car is driven off in an emergency while connected to the pump whether or not a fuel spill will result. It's a matter of the type of equipment in play.

Most people tend to stay outside the car while they fill up. In observing people in the white state of awareness, checking e-mail or texting on their phone while standing by the filler cap or while sitting inside the car seems to be common. Those in yellow state of awareness remain alert. In terms of positioning yourself for surveillance, standing with your back against the car between the hose and the driver's seat is considered more effective than with your back to the pump. This limits the amount of blind spots to deal with.

Another way to spend fill time is to inspect the exterior of the vehicle. At constant risk are the condi-tion of the tires as well as the headlights and taillights. After starting the pump, walking the perimeter of the vehicle will offer additional surveillance opportunities.

As outlined in Chapter 1, the number one reason more precautions are not regularly practiced is because they take extra time. The biggest time consumer in the yellow awareness fuel stop was circling of the premises before stopping at a pump. In reviewing videotapes of several different fuel stops at different locations, driv-ing the perimeter of the typical gas station consumed 30-35 seconds on average when compared to just driving up to the nearest open pump. That's just not very much time considering what may be happening in the duration.

Any time you pull into a gas station there can be predators watching for the purpose of sizing you up and measuring risk versus reward—do you have something they want versus how easy would it be to steal it from you? This is one of the Five Stages of Violent Crime referred to as Interview, where the criminal decides if you are safe to attack. If you can demonstrate strong vigilance and awareness in your mannerisms, you have a better chance of tipping the "how easy would it be" part of the equation in your favor. So would choosing a pump in full view of the front door of the station. This would introduce greater fear of being seen adding to risk. If during your drive around (performing an interview of your own) you can see or merely suspect that you are being sized up, not stopping and going somewhere else is an even better response. Keep in mind that the most important preemptive behavioral response in the fuel stop game is to not be desperate for lack of fuel, forcing you to stop somewhere that you don't feel safe. Don't wait until your gas gauge is on empty.

Being worried about extra time can also make you act in desperation. When we decided to find another gas station because there were as many as five young men waiting by telephones gawking at us like they had nothing else on their minds besides our entrance, all it cost us was time. At another location, our other fuel stop was delayed because we noticed that the premises also seemed to double as a rendezvous for day laborers and employers. As much as we could empathize with the men waiting in need of a job, we thought the incidence of panhandling or other forms of unwanted interaction were inevitable. One stop we should have not made was when we failed to recognize that the car parked at the opposite side of the pump was not actually being filled. The driver remained seated in his car and glared across at us trying to get our attention, calling out "Sir, Sir?" Evidently this was his style of begging for fuel money. Not leaving his car meant he could have had a weapon out of our view. Holding to a strict protocol hovering between yellow and orange awareness, and using body language to openly display our mistrust and willingness to act, we completed our fuel stop and left.

If you are wondering how much longer it takes to perform a fuel stop that is punctuated by a series of "stop, look, and listen" head swivels, you must remember that movement of the head must be accompanied by eyes that are prepared to take in new information. The eyes are the fastest physical coordination we have but you must have a willingness to see and understand what is taking place in the field of view. According to the our video studies, a scan with recognition may only require 2.2 to 2.5 seconds on average.

You can get a feel for how long about two and one-half seconds actually is by verbally repeating one-Mississippi, two-Mississippi. Maybe you learned this technique when you were a kid. If you only had three friends and a football you could still strike up a game of two-hand touch. One guy hiked the football to his quarterback and then ran out for a pass. Your teammate went out to cover the receiver while you stayed behind and counted to three-Mississippi before rushing the quarterback. But just like how fast you count relies on an honor system, you've got to concentrate on focusing around you and relaying information to the brain. Even police and military recruits have fallen into the trap of mere choreography while performing a check-six drill in training (turning to see who or what is behind you), failing to see an assistant drill instructor pointing a dummy gun directly at them.

The elapsed time from the moment you stop at the pump and exit the vehicle is perhaps the most important interval. You are still relatively secure in the vehicle with the doors locked and windows raised. You are not yet tethered to the pump and the engine should still be running so the possibility of escape remains a viable option. Upon reviewing multiple videos of our fuel stops, the elapsed time it takes to complete surveillance from the driver's seat, including the use of the right and left side and rearview mirrors, is approximately twelve to thirteen seconds. Of course, that is if you see nothing out of the ordinary that requires further checking before deciding to get out of the car or leave.

Ultimately, the fuel stop performed in the white state of mind is going to be faster than one performed punctuated by purposeful surveillance and recognition. Unless, of course, the fuel stop is interrupted by an assault or merely being hassled by a panhandler. To help prevent being caught by surprise, punctuate your actions with instances of comprehension and judgment by pacing yourself. Pacing is a method

Answering questions posed by the order screen can be mesmerizing, completely separating your attention from what is going on around you. But this man is pacing himself by punctuating his operation of the keyboard with quick scans of his surroundings. In addition, his demeanor is intimidating rather than timid.

of balancing out moments of distraction or intense concentration with moments of surveillance. For every period of distraction or moment in which you are devoting complete concentration to the chore at hand, there should also be a corresponding period of looking around resulting in genuine recognition of what is before you. The outward appearance of someone who is punctuating or pacing themselves with moments of surveillance should project an attitude bordering on arrogance, thus offering a higher state of awareness to onlookers as a warning.

So, how much longer does it take to begin fueling if the only interruption to the process was the yellow awareness protocol described above? Let's calculate using maximum rather than average elapsed times as our Delta for each visual scan.

Circling the premises before parking	35 seconds
Looking before exiting the automobile	13 seconds
Standing beside the car before stepping to the pump	5 seconds
Scanning left and right during processes before swiping card	2.5 seconds
Answering questions:	
Are you a member?	2.5 seconds
Debit or credit?	2.5 seconds
Enter Zip code	2.5 seconds
Car wash?	2.5 seconds
Do you want a receipt?	2.5 seconds
Total Elapsed Time	68 seconds

If you think you do not have the patience for taking the extra time to perform so many individual scans you are not alone. As a team we were surprised ourselves how little extra time was necessary to increase security many times over. Given the elapsed real time was only about 68 seconds, it's easy to start a campaign for repeated surveillance with the slogan, "It only takes a minute to be safer."

What Case Studies Tell Us

One of the earliest lessons in personal safety passed down from parent to child is to "Look both ways before crossing the street." Another lesson is "Don't take candy from a stranger." How about don't give candy to a stranger. That would be a good example of the White level of awareness.

In June of 2015, a woman parked at a gas station in Houston, Texas, was approached by a man who announced that it was his birthday. He wasn't looking for food but wanted a beer. According to a report on KPRC-TV, the local NBC affiliate, the woman said, "OK, it's your birthday. I'll help you get a beer." But when she opened her purse, the man punched her in the face, took her purse, and ran. All this happened with the woman's two-year old daughter sitting in the back seat.[1]

Part and parcel of the color-coded awareness system is when and where you are. One must ask if the woman were in a bar instead of at a gas station would she have bought a complete stranger a beer? In a bar the woman might have been more judgmental, perhaps wondering if the man considered himself a likely suitor. There is no indication how the man was dressed when he approached the woman at the gas station but if he were in the condition of a panhandler inside the bar wouldn't the woman assume a more defensive posture? The man was captured and held for police by a Good Samaritan who took it upon himself to assume the risk of being injured.

Obviously, the man had sized her up and perhaps the woman was intimidated. The lesson here is to put up a tough front and appear unapproachable, not to mention keeping the doors locked with the windows rolled up. Each of these precautions would not only provide a boundary but also broadcast a yellow or orange state of awareness. Both the woman and her child were at risk of kidnapping. Ultimately a third person was put at risk as well, even if it was by choice.

The incident could likely have been avoided if the gas station was just that, a place to buy gasoline and nothing else. Without the attraction of alcohol sales (or food and cigarettes) there would be little reason for people to congregate beyond the necessity of refueling. Several Crime Stoppers videos reaching out for possible witnesses are available on the Internet. Many include images of perpetrators that moments before the crime were just standing around in front of a convenience store. One such video posted by the Atlanta Police Department in 2013 shows a carjacking and kidnapping. First we see two men clearly walking from in front of the store to the victim, who was parked at the pump furthest from the camera and the front of the store. The two men split up, approaching from behind the pump on the opposite side from the victim. One perpetrator comes at the victim from the front of the car and other from the rear corner. Police said one man pulled a gun and ordered the victim back into his car. He was driven to a location and robbed.[2]

Another type of crime typically perpetrated by loiterers is referred to as "sliding." Sliding is a crime of stealth that could be described as pickpocketing your car. The thief, now commonly referred to as the "slider" looks for cars with open windows and any sort of valuables, preferably a purse, left on the seat. The slider crouches or crawls closely along the passenger side of the car beneath eye level while the victim is refueling. He or she then reaches up through the

Many Crime Stoppers videos, which are in effect pleas to the public for witnesses to come forward, show that robberies and kidnappings are more likely to occur at pumps located furthest from the front door of the gas station or convenience store. The card readers located at the station's outer perimeter are also more likely to be fit with a skimming device to steal credit or debit card information. It's no wonder why this pump facing away from the front door and closest to the street shows the most abuse.

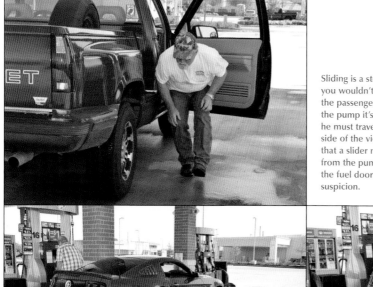

Sliding is a stealth method of theft that takes place at a gas station, but you wouldn't know it from the image of the man crouching as he exits the passenger side of the vehicle. His truck is parked so far away from the pump it's not even in the picture. This serves to reduce the distance he must travel to the target vehicle as he "slides" up to the passenger side of the victim's car and reaches inside the window. The first clue that a slider may be lying in wait is a vehicle parked inordinately distant from the pumps. In addition, any time you see a vehicle parked with the fuel door on the opposite side from the pump should also raise suspicion.

open window and removes the item, then moves away crouching so as not to be seen.

Sliders can also work with an accomplice. They arrive in a car and park near the pump on the opposite island, acting as if they are going to get gas. But the slider car is usually parked further away from the pump than normal. This position is to provide visual cover as the passenger (who may be slouching down in the seat) gets out and moves below eye level to the open car window. If you see a car parked further away than normal while you are refueling, you should be suspicious and make sure your windows are up. You can also move to another pump. When you get out of the car use the electronic lock to keep all the doors secure. Let yourself out by manually unlocking the driver's side door only.

In July of 2013, NBCSanDiego.com reported that a man that tried to kidnap a woman at a gas station in Chula Vista had been arrested. The story begins with a key phrase reading, "A man caught on surveillance tape . . ."[3] Indeed, many people feel safe because of the presence of video surveillance. However, it is also very common for perpetrators to cover their faces.

Video surveillance is more often thought of as contributing to evidence in an investigation after the fact. But it's much better to survive an attack and serve as a corroborating witness in aiding the capture

Walking around the vehicle to check the condition of the tires is a habit that can protect you from a breakdown on the road. So is taking wide turns at each corner. This vantage point gives the car owner plenty of time to react beyond the reach of a slider who may react violently upon discovery.

and prosecution of the attacker. That's exactly what happened in the Chula Vista case because the victim didn't give up.

According to a report by the Chula Vista Police Department, on July 14, 2013, at around 11:50 p.m., Thomas Paciornik entered the lot of the 7-Eleven station on Hilltop Drive and Orange Avenue, stopping his car near to the victim's vehicle. He introduced himself as Tom and told her she was pretty. He asked her to go with him. She refused and got inside her own car. Paciornik, who later pled guilty to felony attempted kidnapping among other charges, tried to remove her from her car, grabbing her by arm and kissing her. Enraged by failing to remove her from her car, Pacriornik returned to his own vehicle and backed into the front of the victim's car in order to prevent her from driving forward. In addition, he punctured one of the woman's tires and reportedly told her that she had five seconds to get into his car.

The woman refused again and Paciornik left the scene. But when the victim pulled her car into a parking stall at the gas station, Paciornik returned and parked his vehicle so that the woman was not able to open her driver's side door. When witnesses began yelling that police were on the way, Paciornik finally fled the scene.

The perpetrator was tracked via the license plate visible on the surveillance video but not to his home.

Instead, Paciornik was arrested after being involved in yet another incident. After the attempted abduction at the gas station, he subsequently valet-parked at the Viejas Casino in Alpine. Police were called to a disturbance when Paciornik was unable to claim the vehicle due to improper documentation. Initially arrested for being under the influence of a controlled substance, good police work tied him to the assault at the gas station.[4]

Video surveillance can be effective only if the camera can pick up features of personal identification and/or a license plate number. This often requires the proper camera angle. The victim was able to provide key points of identification such as marks on his face that added to the veracity of the video because she survived. She survived because she did not give up. That her resistance caused the action of the crime to shift from one side of the gas station to another likely played a part in providing the camera with the necessary angle to capture the license plate number as well as the perpetrator's image and any smaller detail that would help identify the perpetrator or his car. While the victim's continued resistance almost gave police enough time to reach the scene, the actions of the resistance also alerted witnesses whose pronouncement of the police being on the way short-circuited the attack and likely prevented an escalation of violence.

Preemptive Behavioral Response at the Gas Station

Checklist

Refuel regularly to avoid running low on fuel.

Pick a station that only sells fuel to reduce the amount of loitering.

Avoid stations that sell alcohol.

Avoid stations that serve as a meeting place for day laborers.

Choose a station that is well lit.

Circle the station before stopping to see who is watching you.

If you are being surveilled, leave the premises.

Check for anyone hanging around for no apparent reason.

If there are people loitering, leave the premises.

Be suspicious of cars parked too far from the pump.

Choose a pump that is in view of the cashier or the front door.

Before exiting the vehicle, look around just as if you were changing lanes on a highway.

Make sure your windows are up.

Unlock only the driver's side door when exiting.

Upon exiting the vehicle, stand and look around before approaching the pump.

If you are paying cash, walk directly inside. Tell the clerk what number pump you intend to use. If you are not filling up the tank, hand the clerk the exact change without announcing the dollar amount.

Always use the credit option on your debit card to avoid exposing your personal identification number. If you must use a debit card with PIN number, go inside the store.

Before swiping your card, inspect the condition of the card reader for damage, even as minor as scratches.

Inspect the seal on the card reader for tampering or multiple layers.

When charging at the pump, do not let anyone approach you while operating the credit card reader.

When using a credit card, punctuate fulfillment of the commands with looking left and right, behind you, and across to the opposite side of the pump.

If you remain outside the car, stand with your back against the vehicle or walk around the vehicle to inspect the tires.

Do not use your cell phone while refueling, whether you remain standing or sitting inside the car.

Chapter 4 What Everyone Can Learn from Professional Drivers

Outside of just a few big cities with large networks of public transportation, driving a car in America is a necessity. So it shouldn't come as a surprise that according to the Federal Highway Administration there are more than 214 million drivers currently licensed in the United States alone.[1] Our love affair with cars (and trucks) is just part of being an American, and for many young people driving represents not only independence but also a coming of age. Driving professionally may or may not be considered skilled labor because it's taking advantage of something most of us already do. But for many American citizens it is their first adult job that earns enough to start a family or put themselves through college.

It's no secret that many immigrants begin their lives in America by driving a taxicab. A good driver with minimal education can earn money quickly with little or no investment. Yet, in many cultures around the world, segments of the population, specifically women, are not permitted to drive nor are they allowed to work. In America, the freedom to be licensed to drive opens up new possibilities for making a living.

Commuting to work, school, or simply running errands can make you feel like driving is a fulltime job but it is the professional driver that logs many, many, more miles transporting people and valuable goods both locally and border to border. In most cases their vehicles are branded with signs that can just as easily draw thieves as attract new customers. That being said, a study of lessons learned by cabbies should yield valuable insights into personal defense for everyone that drives.

For the driver of a private, unmarked vehicle, there are places where you go that can be just as dangerous as driving a vehicle with signage. Anytime you visit a bank or use a drive-up ATM, your risk of being the victim of a crime skyrockets. Expensive commodities such as computers and flat screen TVs are difficult to hide but easy to sell if they are stolen. In either case, all a criminal has to do is set up in front of a bank or computer store and follow the victim when they leave. If your next stop is someplace like the dry cleaners, the thieves can simply clean out your car while you are inside picking up your clothes. The underworld community has even come up with a name for this method of crime. It's called "Jugging." Another bad end result to a shopping trip can be a driveway robbery in which you're followed home and attacked in your driveway or garage while unloading.

Cars can be easily broken into when left unattended, but the real danger is when the crime involves personal contact and not just theft, such as in the case of a carjacking, the preferred method for many car thieves because with the driver present and the engine running there is no need to damage the car to gain entry and drive off. The risk of confronting the driver and/or passengers is often outweighed by the reward of a new automobile fully intact, especially when you take into account the advantage of surprise and how difficult it is to mount a defense from the confines of the interior of an automobile. In this regard, both professional drivers and private drivers face similar risks.

Unfortunately, the professional driver operates in a world where risk versus reward is much more heavily loaded at both ends of the equation. The goods an over-the-road (OTR) freight driver carries up the reward. The local delivery driver makes many stops, often parking the vehicle where it is subject to theft. Pizza delivery personnel are walking cash registers approaching complete strangers while separated from their vehicle. The taxi cab driver knows little or nothing about their passengers and taxi driver's earnings mount up as the shift continues, boosting the reward for theft. The limousine driver may also be carrying cash and the image of opulence can be a signal that whoever is in the back seat is rich and replete with valuables. Before formulating a list of safety precautions for the private driver, let's take a look at how each of these professional drivers operate and find out what preemptive behavioral responses have been developed by the professionals.

Taxi Cabs, Limousines, and Private Hire Transport

The yellow cab taxi is the most well known image of personal transport, but not all taxis are painted yellow. Yellow is the traditional color because it stands out in traffic, making the cabs easily seen by anyone who needs to hire them. The fact that the taxi wants to be noticed stands out not only in traffic but also within

Are you safer in a taxi? The traditional yellow taxi cab is a highly regulated industry charging standardized rates for distance and waiting time that do not vary as if their services were a commodity rising and falling with market demands. This begins with a properly-calibrated meter checked and maintained by the fleets and inspected by the licensing bureau. Unlike some independent transport entities, taxi drivers are fingerprinted and go through a thorough background check by local police or taxi and limousine commission.

the transport industry itself. While the taxi cab can be hired over the telephone or pick up fares (passenger or passengers) by waiting on line at an airport, bus station, hotel, or other point of heavy demand, the most traditional way a taxi driver makes his living is by stopping for anyone that hails them from the curb. The risk is obvious.

The primary job of all personal transport drivers is to simply pick up passengers from one location and deliver them to another. But from the moment a shift begins to the time it ends, driving a taxicab is a completely unique experience. First, let's consider the different ways in which the business is structured. The cabs themselves are licensed by the city and/or state to perform livery service within specific guidelines. A "medallion" is physically affixed to the vehicle itself, usually on the hood. A metering device inspected and sealed is attached to the cab to register distance driven and time elapsed once activated for service. A taxi may at times be hired for a flat rate but the meter is the primary source of charges per trip. A light on the roof of the cab indicates when the cab is off duty, when the meter is running with a passenger in charge, and when the cab is available for hire. When the cab is available for hire, the driver cannot by rule refuse a fare unless the person or persons is under the influence or demonstrably violent. There are exceptions regarding the distance or radius in which a cab can pick up fares, but in general the driver must take them wherever they request. Most of the rides are relatively short because the taxi is a conveyance of convenience above all else. In my two-year career as a yellow cab driver I never left the boroughs of Manhattan, Brooklyn, Queens, or the Bronx, yet I racked up over 3,000 miles of driving per year.

The requirements for cab drivers are relatively few but specific licensing does include a fingerprint and background check. There is also a written test based primarily on traffic law and knowledge of the city. Driving a cab may be risky but it is a way to make money quickly with few educational requirements.

But making money as a cab driver is not as simple as it sounds, beginning with how your paycheck is accounted. Traditionally, a driver would work for a cab company that maintains a fleet of taxis. Like the popular television show *Taxi* that ran from 1978 into the next decade, the drivers showed up and were assigned a cab to drive for the designated shift. There was a twelve-hour day shift and twelve-hour night shift with the start time assigned by the fleet or cab owner. The driver then was paid a percentage of the meter charges during the shift plus cash tips. The percentage of the meter charges paid to the driver increased with tenure. This was the condition of the taxi industry I personally experienced during my first tenure behind the wheel in the 1970s.

When I returned to taxi driving a decade later, I didn't stay long because the business had changed dramatically. I had heard tales of drivers making much more money by leasing the cabs per shift instead of working for a fleet and sharing the meter. I soon found out that leasing per shift instead of splitting the meter may have increased the maximum amount a driver could take in but it also made the drivers more desperate. This dramatically changed conditions on the road. Fees for driving the day shift could be more than $100 and double that for a night shift ride. This was reflected in a November 2011 Forbes.com article titled "How Taxi Companies Rip Off Their Drivers" by Marc Weber Tobias.[2] Hourly wages commonly worked out to as little as eight dollars or less. But Tobias points out another hazard, collecting wages for fares paid by credit cards. In my time of experience with leasing it was an all cash business. Drivers in the twenty-first century might have to wait weeks for their shares from credit card purchases but still pay every day for their shifts. The immediate effect in the opinion of my peers was that the need to recoup and profit encouraged more aggressive driving. The one aspect of our safety that we had complete control over, our own behavior behind the wheel, was being eroded by acts of desperation.

In Chapter 2, we saw that being desperate can negatively affect judgment. In addition, competition with other drivers was more likely to lead to violence. It wasn't uncommon for drivers to cut each other off to reach passengers waiting at the curb, leading to fender benders. In a city like New York where sidewalks are filled with pedestrians overflowing into the streets, a car out of control could prove deadly. Fights between drivers were beginning to be a problem, too.

Might a cabbie desperate to recoup his lease payment then take a fare they might ordinarily avoid? We already pointed out that any time the available light is lit the driver cannot refuse a fare. But the driver does have the right to go off duty and may do so immediately upon delivering a passenger to their destination. For example, most taxi drivers will not take a fare to a part of a given city that is well known to have a high crime rate. This does not mean that everyone who lives there is a criminal. Nor does it mean that residents of higher crime neighborhoods do not need or desire cab service. In fact, it could be seen as just the opposite. Yet it may be difficult for a passenger bound for rundown or crime-ridden streets to ask a cabbie straight out to take them far from downtown and share in the predicament in which they live.

For example, after dropping a fare in lower Manhattan I was hailed by an older woman who looked like she'd been working a double shift at one of the stifling little factories dug in between the tenements not far from the Brooklyn Bridge. I asked her where she was going and the lady answered cautiously in the way an immigrant who could barely speak English would respond. Seated in the cab I could see she was probably about sixty years old, overweight, and probably pretty tired. Clutching her black patent leather purse, she half nodded and half pointed with both hands on the purse mumbling, "Just over the bridge." I flipped the flag down to start the meter and headed across into Brooklyn. With the bridge a few blocks behind us, I half turned and half looked into the rearview mirror asking, "Stop here?" She

pointed again with her hands in front of her chest holding her purse as if they were the reigns of a horse-drawn carriage signaling "a little further." We continued to ride deeper into Brooklyn.

To look at us both we were two people at different ends of the spectrum. She may have been an immigrant from Jamaica, very dark-skinned and much older than myself. I was of course white, male, only in my twenties, and reveled in looking like a hoodlum. My soft eyes might have given me away but driving a cab and living on the Lower East Side did require some sort of armor. I asked again and again; she responded each time by saying something like "further," "more," or just pointed. When we arrived at our destination some fifty minutes later, I realized that she did indeed speak English, but in my opinion was ashamed not of her language skills but of the neighborhood in which she lived. Actually, halfway into the trip I understood what was happening and wondered where we would end up. If she had asked to go to East New York, Brooklyn, right away most cabbies would not have done so. Along the way I reasoned that if she could live there, I could go there. Even if my cab did stick out like a neon sign saying "rob me please" of the eighty or so dollars in small bills I had pressed beneath my thigh against the driver's seat. This was the same East New York, Brooklyn neighborhood policed by NYPD detective Derrick Parker, "NYPD's First 'Hip Hop' Cop" in his book, *Notorious C.O.P.* A sign at his place of business, the 75th Precinct, was a satire of the slogan used by 1010 WINS News Radio, "You give us 22 minutes, we'll give you the world." The sign read, "You give us 22 minutes, we'll give you a homicide."[3] In 2007, the *Village Voice* rated East New York, Brooklyn as the best place to get murdered, raped, or robbed.

My point is that a driver desperate to make up for an exorbitant lease fee might not have immediately turned off his available light upon delivering his or her passenger before being accosted. The prospect of driving so far back to Manhattan without the meter running might have tempted the desperate driver to take the very next fare no matter who they might be or where they were going. I turned on my off-duty light and, fascinated by the scene of people living amidst the devastation of burned-out buildings, vacant lots, gated and barricaded small shops, took a few turns through the neighborhood and got the hell out.

Changing your status light to off-duty immediately upon delivery of a passenger can be a lifesaver. Or, at least provide an excuse not to pick someone up that you do not want to take on. As such, here is a good example. A driver picks up a fare headed for a specific address on Seventh Avenue in Manhattan (New York City). He writes the address in his logbook and pulls out into traffic. The passenger is from out of town and has never been to this address before let alone the "Fashion District," a stretch of blocks just below 42nd Street where Seventh Avenue is officially referred to as Fashion Avenue. The buildings are largely occupied by importers of clothing and others doing business in the textile industry. The streets are absolutely teeming with pedestrians crossing illegally, "jaywalking" at all angles. Workers pushing racks of clothing and large plastic bins filled with cloth are common sights. As the cab crosses 42nd Street headed south, the driver is looking carefully for the address above each doorway. Manhattan is a grid system of streets crossing at 90 degree angles with few exceptions. There are twenty streets or rather blocks to a mile and the driver is trying to find the address based on how the numbers correspond to each block. He finds the correct address, pulls over to the right hand side of the avenue, and stops his meter. The driver collects the fare in cash and the passenger gets out. As the passenger leaves, the driver writes the time of arrival in his logbook. He looks up from his writing and that's when trouble begins.

There is a limousine parked in front of the building with a uniformed chauffeur standing beside it. Here is what the chauffeur sees. The cab approaches with

the driver bending forward to get a better look at the building's address. He stops and sits back, reaching towards the passenger to accept payment and make change. The passenger leaves and although the driver is double-parked and blocking traffic, he remains parked while writing something down. The light on his taxi indicates he is available and a wiry, rough-looking young man taps on the driver's window. The young man tries to get into the passenger seat but the door is locked. It's pretty obvious he wants to hire the cab but the driver does not want to take him. The argument escalates and as the driver goes to put the cab into gear the man jumps on the hood. The argument continues through the windshield. The man balls his fist and delivers a blow to the hood, actually leaving a bowl-shaped dent. The driver puts the cab in gear, accelerates and stops short, throwing the man off the hood. He then takes off again but runs down a pedestrian instead, hitting a man pushing a clothes rack. The clothes go into the street with the rack skittering in one direction and the pedestrian rolling and sliding towards the curb. He ends up lying prone in front of the parked limousine, badly injured. The young man who wanted to hire the cab disappears but an angry crowd gathers. The cab is surrounded and the chauffeur has to fend off attacks by members of the lynch mob who arrive late and assume based on the position of the victim that it was the limo that had run him down. Police and ambulance arrive with the taxi driver locked inside his cab with the windows up and the chauffeur fending off attacks and pinning a man to the hood of the limo in a hammerlock.

Several factors contributed to the debacle, not the least of which was the time period (the 1970s) and the way in which people hired taxicabs. Back then, almost all passengers were picked up from the street by catching the eye of the cabbie. Another problem for the cabbie was having to look for an exact address and not understanding the grid system of blocks and streets. By knowing the proper cross street, such as 38th Street and Seventh Avenue, the driver would have been less distracted. While the passenger did not in fact know the location of the address, the driver should have tried to get permission to drop the fare at the nearest corner or ask them to look above each doorway themselves to find the address. It's better to overshoot the address than take your eyes off the road to find it. Switching his off-duty light on directly upon arrival at the destination would have given the driver an opportunity to evaluate his surroundings. At the very least the driver could have driven off as soon as the door closed and entered the time of delivery the next time he stopped. As for the limousine driver, it was a case of being in the wrong place at the wrong time.

Taxicab driving will always be a higher-risk job than the norm. The leasing of cabs per shift is still prevalent but communications technology has done much to change the business by making the dispatch team a much more important resource for the driver. For example, until cell phones replaced the pager and became commonplace, drivers either cruised the streets or waited in queue at taxi stands by a railroad terminal or at the airport. The driver rarely called dispatch unless there was a flat tire, an accident, or a mechanical breakdown. It's still profitable to rely on being hailed street-side in big cities like New York or Chicago, but more fares are booked directly by cell phone or text message than ever before.

The in-cab camera has proven to be a huge boost to security for the driver. Beyond the obvious surety of visual proof, the camera can also function as an early warning system. If a prospective fare shows reluctance to enter the cab but engages the driver in prolonged conversation they may be trying to commit a robbery without running the risk of sitting in the cab and being identified.

The in-cab computer allows for the driver to respond quickly to calls without the exposure of cruising the streets. Once in the computer, requests for service are more likely to be recorded and kept on file and there's a built-in GPS that can trace the whereabouts of the cab at any given time. Electronic payment removes the lure of ready cash.

Several attempts have been made to prevent crimes against taxi drivers. Two of the most recognizable are the addition of a safe that is accessible only to the cab owner or fleet cashier and the bullet-resistant partition. Another deterrent is the installation of a surveillance camera.

Installing a safe and displaying a decal such as "Driver only carries $X in change" or "Driver cannot access safe" will make potential criminals aware that the amount of funds available to them are limited. How effective is this strategy? A safe probably does reduce the probability of crime because criminals are usually looking for the easiest victim. However, the veracity of the decals might come into question since

not every holdup man is going to take the driver's word for it. Before the installation of safes, taxicab drivers used several methods of deception to minimize loss. Years ago, drivers generally divided up the take during each shift in either one of two strategies. They would hide large bills or a predetermined amount of money somewhere in the cab. Single dollar bills and fives were change money so they were kept in supply. A maximum of two or three twenty-dollar bills might be kept in different pockets. Or, the driver might keep a separate wallet beneath their leg. Some drivers liked having a cigar box next to them as a cash register. This made change convenient but served as a smoke screen. The idea was to divert attention to the cigar box. Another favorite ploy was the "chump roll," a roll or wad of cash made up of mostly single dollar bills with a twenty-dollar bill or even a phony fifty on the outside. In the event of a holdup, the plan was to throw the chump roll out the window and drive off.

When we think of risk to taxicab drivers, pressure-cooker cities like the five boroughs of New York City come to mind. Oddly enough, one of the greater forces pushing for use of the partition came from a 1991 set of reports and recommendations by the Manitoba Taxicab Board. The Canadian province of Manitoba is centrally located directly above the borders of North Dakota and Minnesota. The governmental and cultural center of the province is the city of Winnipeg, serviced by a vibrant taxicab industry. As such, the Manitoba Taxicab Board was alarmed by violence against taxicab drivers that translated into some rather frightening statistics. Based on statistics published in the American Journal of Public Health in October, 1987, "the work related homicide rate for Winnipeg cab drivers (50 per 100,000) computed to about two-and-a-half times the rate for both cab drivers and policemen in California; the same as the rate for inmates in U.S. Federal prisons; and twenty-four times the rate for all male workers in Texas."[4]

The installation of a bullet-resistant partition separating the driver from the rear is currently mandatory in New York City but its use has periodically been both in and out of favor with drivers and passengers alike. Passengers didn't like it because it pretty much killed the conversation with the driver. (Talking sports and politics with a cab driver is considered part of the New York experience.) It also interfered with giving instructions to the driver and making payment. Often the partition was slid aside in frustration by the driver and left that way.

The history of safety partitions can be traced back to 1960 when, after a rash of fatal armed robberies of cab drivers, the NYPD gave cab owners permission to install clear partitions to deter holdups. In 1967, the city required bullet-resistant partitions in cabs driven at night. By 1971, all cabs were required to have partitions, and in that same year the New York Taxi and Limousine Commission (TLC) was formed, relieving the police department from regulation. Current TLC regulation 67-10 (a) (1) requires the use of a partition that "isolates the driver from the rear seat passengers or all passengers of the vehicle."[5] This forbids carriage of passengers in the front seat. Regulation 67-10 (a) (2) states, "The purpose of the partition is to provide protection to the driver while ensuring passenger safety and enabling rear seat passengers to enjoy a clear and unobstructed view of the Taxicab Driver's License, Rate Card, and front windshield."[6]

The list of complaints about using a partition is long. Communication is stifled. The partitions themselves are unsightly, difficult to clean, and subject to vandalism such as graffiti both by writing and by scratching into the plastic. Riders don't generally like them because they feel they've been put in a cage or riding in the back of a police car. The partition can also prove injurious in the case of a sudden stop. "Those partitions create a plastic surgeon's dream," said Jack S. Lusk, New York TLC chairman from 1988 to 1991. In the very same article published in 2005 on YellowCabNYCTaxi.com, Fidel F. Del Valle, who was the commission's chairman from 1991 to 1995 countered by saying, "The attractiveness of robbing a cab is that it's basically a piggy bank on wheels. You don't want to make the opportunity for crime any easier than it is."[7]

An exemption from the requirement to use a partition can be found in the New York TLC code Section 5, subsection 58-35 (b) (1), requiring the cab to be driven by the owner of the Medallion. What's more interesting is an exemption commonly found across the nation. While some commissions still require the use of a partition for the night shift, the presence of an interior camera can in some precincts release the cab driver and/or cab owner from the requirement of having a safety partition. For anyone thinking of buying into the cab business with a fleet or even a single car, it is recommended to study the laws and regulations in the city in which you will be setting up shop. If you are considering being a driver, contact one or more fleets that are looking for drivers. They'll be able to tell you what the physical requirements of each cab are and of course their cabs will be equipped as such. But questions remain about the variation in safety requirements and what equipment and conditions have the greatest effect on safety.

Results from a wide cross section of interviews with working cab drivers revealed that advancements in technology have had a more positive effect on driver safety than that of physical barriers. You can never discount street smarts but the almost-complete disappearance of cash payment is perhaps the greatest deterrent to crime, second only to the vast reduction in the amount of fares picked up at random rather than by cell phone, including transit apps such as HAIL A CAB.

Let's take some representative cab rides to find out what driving in today's taxicab industry is all about.

If you're not willing or able to call in a request for pickup, the quickest way to get a cab is to find a cabstand where they wait in queue. The most typical location is around the corner from a large hotel. If it were twenty years ago, the drivers would be standing outside their cabs smoking and trading stories. Today, they sit in their cars looking at a touch screen where jobs are being posted continuously. They continue to wait on line or respond electronically for the job and leave the other drivers to wait. To save wear on their fingertips, several drivers on line were using a small remote to choose a pickup close to their immediate location or delete it from the screen.

Most of the drivers waiting to be called to the front of the hotel by the doorman or bell captain were looking for a substantial fare such as a ride to the airport. It may be difficult to comprehend but years ago the fleet would gas up the cab for you free of charge. Today's leasing cabbies have to factor in fuel costs, so the driver

has to weigh spending downtime versus intermittent trips to the airport that guarantee a higher fee plus extra for handling baggage. That's why for a ride crosstown, only a cab at the very back of the line was willing to take my fare. My destination was the Harris County (Texas) criminal court located at the opposite side of town. I chose the court district because its high volume of foot traffic would hopefully provide the best opportunity to hail a cab the old-fashioned way, with a wave of the hands.

With a sticker showing a maximum crosstown rate of six dollars, it was no wonder only a backmarker on the line was willing to take me. This was obviously an attempt at getting more people to use taxicabs. Another sticker on the passenger window said the driver only has two dollars in cash. The driver was from Nigeria and has been driving a cab for three years. When asked why there were no partitions in any of the cabs, he said he would prefer one for night shift. But there was a surveillance camera mounted above the rearview mirror staring me in the face. His least favorite times to work were Friday and Saturday nights even though they could be the most lucrative. Why? Because of drunks. By law, drivers are not required to transport people under the influence but it's not always possible to identify the inebriated before they get into the cab and the meter has started. This part of driving a cab will never change.

For the next ride, I waited outside the bustling courthouse for about twenty minutes before one lone yellow cab was visible in traffic. I hailed it and the driver pulled over. The taxi was a somewhat aged minivan with sliding door access to the passenger compartment. Unfortunately, the door handle didn't work properly. The driver had to exit the vehicle and open the door for me. The interior of the cab was not partitioned but again, an interior surveillance camera was watching.

Once inside the cab, I found that the driver was of classic description. Not merely engaging, he began

Hail a Cab apps (applications) have made taxi driving a much more secure profession. Certainly anyone bent on robbing a cab driver can order a cab on a borrowed or stolen cell phone to avoid being traced, but with so many riders now using their smart phones, the much more dangerous method of cruising the streets for fares is nearly nonexistent.

asking me about my background in a thick accent. Driving on and off since 1983, he owned the cab outright but the medallion was mortgaged. His least favorite passengers were teenagers or young adults. He said that he'd been robbed twice. Given he had exited the cab and was out of view of the security camera inside his cab I was pretty sure he'd be robbed again. Sure, the street scene where he picked me up was amidst a throng of people in front of a criminal courts building, but what about the next time he was making a pickup on an empty street?

He described one robbery as being by a professional yet no money was taken. It was strictly of the "gun to the head and apology for not having money for the fare" variety. The driver referred to the situation as being professional because he saw the incident as part and parcel of the man's lifestyle. One might compare it to a scofflaw offense such as jumping a subway turnstile. The definition of the word scofflaw shares terminology with the word outlaw, "one who habitually ignores the law."

Dealing with riders skipping out on the fare will always be a part of driving a cab. Surveillance cameras inside the cab may make it less likely but it's never a good idea to run after a fare beater. First of all, you lose control of the cab and what's inside. Second, you are away from your own security camera and whatever happens will likely not be witnessed. If they have a weapon they are more likely to use it outside the cab. The point of departure may in fact be on "their turf" and have help readily available. The amount of money lost to fare abandonment is further tempered by the leasing agreement since the cab owner will not be sharing in your take, whereas in the old days the cab owner shared in your take, so a lost fare should not in itself result in a calamitous loss of income.

The second robbery he described was, in his words, actually lucky for him but really couldn't happen today. In the 1980s, when cash was the only method of payment, there was a rash of taxicab robberies by

the same man. As the fare exited the cab, he reached in and grabbed all the money he could from the cigar/ cash box. The cabbie opened the door, smashing into the thief just as a police car was turning the corner. When the cabbie told the police the robber had taken all his money, the police searched him and removed every cent from his pockets. Fortunately for the cabbie, this included all the money he had taken from each of the previous holdups he had committed. If this story sounds far-fetched, you might chalk it up to how much fun it is to ride in a taxicab and hear good stories. The important point to remember is that if you limit your response to curbside hailing and focus primarily on taking assignments (and payment) electronically, driving a cab is a lot safer than it used to be.

Other robberies related to me through a series of interviews nationwide closely reflect new stories found on the Internet. Two such examples that fit a common MO (modus operandi or method of operation or procedure) begin with how the cab is brought to the scene. Some rides are ordered and even billed through an account attached to a given cell phone. Others, when ordered over a cell phone, are paid via credit card by the passenger at the end of the ride. In the first example, the target of the theft was not the driver or his cash but the taxicab itself. The call was placed on a restaurant telephone so the caller was anonymous. Without a tracking device implanted on the vehicle it was impossible to trace before being disposed of in whole or in pieces.

In another type of robbery, the cab is either hailed at a location with few witnesses or again called in on a telephone not belonging to the perpetrator. (This is a good reason to not let a stranger borrow your cell phone no matter what their tale of woe.) The end result of one such incident as related to me was that the cabbie was shot through the driver's side window as he tried to drive off. To me this begged further explanation, which ultimately revealed how thieves work around the presence of a security camera.

Let's go back and work through the MO of this robbery and some of the options available to the perpetrator. Booked using a third-party phone to a destination with few if any witnesses, the passenger exits the cab before paying, stealing from the cabbie at gunpoint through the driver's side window. That's allegedly what happened in this case. Why wouldn't the perpetrator start the robbery while still inside the cab? The simple answer is because he was under the eye of a security camera. Why didn't he just wear a disguise, sunglasses, hat, or nondescript clothing? Because any attempt capable of obscuring his or her identity would have raised suspicion from the driver and he may have been refused service. Furthermore, while inside the cab the driver can drive off with him aboard. Although I've not actually heard of a verifiable incident of this, every taxi and limousine driver I've ever known said they'd crash the cab, flinging the robber forward while they remained buckled safely in their seats.

Just as an obvious disguise can send up a red flag, so can the actions of a passenger showing surprise and acting uncomfortable in front of a security camera. In the chapter on security for real estate agents we discussed identifying the client and how probing questions can be put in a humorous manner. If the driver is having second thoughts about their passenger, he or she could ask them what they do for a living. If they don't say movie actor offer to send them a copy of the ride as a screen test. Or joke with them about being on the television program *Taxicab Confessions*.

One red flag you really have to be on your toes for is a reluctance to enter the cab. It's a tough one because you have to decide if it's a legitimate concern on their part due to what it might cost or are they working up the nerve to commit a robbery right there to avoid getting into the cab and being recorded by the surveillance camera. We all know what it feels like to make a decision to buy or not to buy. This is a lower-stress situation than pumping up to commit a crime. Look for clenching and unclenching of hands, constriction

of the neck/throat muscles, sweating, or stuttering. It may be a rule that you can't turn down a reasonable request for service but your rule number one, as per the owner/driver described earlier who began his career more than thirty years ago, is "If you don't like how they look, drive off!"

The electronic age of Hail a Cab may have made driving a cab much safer than it used to be but there are still some drawbacks. The lure of quick money doesn't necessarily apply because with payment of fares processed through a credit card or billable account commissions are not distributed on a daily basis. Tips are also counted as part of the pay and rarely given in cash at the end of the ride. This can be a positive if you are trying to save money because the temptation to spend cash tips is much less or even nonexistent. In addition, not walking away from the garage with pockets bulging with small bills greatly reduces the probability of being robbed on the way home from a shift.

One of the questions I was able to ask drivers working in cities where they have the option of legally carrying a concealed firearm was, "Do you carry?" Actually, not every state allows drivers that are also concealed handgun licensees to carry on duty. It is also the prerogative of private companies located in such states to forbid the carriage of a firearm or other types of weapons while driving their cabs. Certainly fleet garages that still operate in the loaning of cabs without the drivers working as independent contractors have the final say. But according to the Houston cabbies that I spoke with operating entirely via a lease program, concealed carry was a real possibility. Of course, this would assume the driver was otherwise qualified under the law. Nevertheless, not one of the cab drivers interviewed actually had or admitted to having a firearm while driving. In some cases this may have had to do with their immigration status, directly or indirectly, even though the background check in Houston, for example, was much the same as for obtaining a CHL, concealed handgun license. The indirect effect of immigration status might simply be that in most countries the population is not allowed to possess firearms, let alone carry them in public, and personal armament is simply a foreign concept, so to speak.

One driver I spoke with said he'd feel safer if he knew that his customers were not able to legally carry a gun. In that case, I pointed out, only the criminals would have guns. Sheepishly, he admitted to keeping a BB gun with him on the job. He explained that he kept it as a deterrent, openly fearing the complications of carrying a deadly weapon more than he feared a situation where he would be unable to scare off a genuine threat. Leaving him to his decision, I would point out to the reader that less than lethal devices should never take on the appearance of actual deadly weapons. We see it in the news all the time. Tragedy instigated by the deployment of a fake gun rendering the use of deadly force by someone with a real gun ending in tragedy.

If there is any doubt about just how much electronic hailing has changed the taxicab profession, consider the following. After a day of interviewing cabbies and riding from one cab stand to another I decided to return to the hotel at my point of origin by manually hailing a cab in the street. Standing on a corner just a block or two off the exit of a freeway feeding traffic back into the downtown area, a lone cab appeared after about a ten-minute wait. Incredibly, it was the same cab I had hailed earlier in front of the courthouse and was in fact the only cab I'd seen the entire day that was working the streets.

Preemptive Behavioral Response for the Taxicab Driver

Checklist

If your impression of the person or persons hailing your cab from the street makes you uncomfortable in any way, keep driving and don't take the fare.

If a radio call or other form of electronic hail brings you to a passenger or to a location that makes you uncomfortable in any way, keep driving and don't take the fare.

Limit or eliminate altogether the practice of picking up passengers via curbside hail.

Don't be afraid to specialize:

Pick up passengers from cabstands directly related to airports or hotels only.

Pick up passengers by radio call or electronic hail only.

Always ask for a cross street to help find an address. Minimize the distraction of looking for an exact address.

Post window stickers such as "Driver only carries $X in change."

Install a bullet-resistant partition and maintain its clarity and all moving parts.

Install a security camera whether or not you have a partition.

Post a sticker alerting the presence of a security camera on all side and rear windows.

Criminals rely on not being identified and prefer to act off-camera. Bear in mind that the moment before a passenger enters the cab and after they exit are critical times.

Be wary of any prospective passenger who appears reluctant to enter the cab.

Do not have an extended conversation with fares outside the cab.

Maintain all doors so the passengers can handle them easily without your assistance.

Maintain the remote door locking feature of your cab.

Enter and/or exit the cab by unlocking only the driver's side door to prevent unwanted intrusion.

Maintain the air conditioning and heating features so the windows need not be opened.

Limousine Driving

Making money driving for a limousine company can mean driving a luxury sedan or even a small motor coach or van. While some fleets specializing in short hauls could be thought of as unmarked upscale taxis, the traditional job of driving a limousine involves both transporting and waiting for clients as they travel to and from airports, shopping trips, business meetings, and special events. With the high-end luxury car driver in mind, here are some tips every professional should know.

The services of a limousine or limousine company are rarely if ever secured without a standing account and/or backing of a credit card. As such, cash is not typically paid directly to the driver. This reduces motivation for robbery but there are still other attractions for the criminal. Instead of money the car itself may be the target. Stolen vehicles are commonly used in other crimes but limos are not a good choice for a getaway car. They are useful to chop shops, however. A chop shop is a garage that specializes in the precision dismantling of stolen cars so that the parts can be sold separately. Whereas a new car depreciates in value the moment it is driven off the dealer's lot, this same car can be sold for much more than its original price tag when sold piece by piece. Some cars are even stolen for a single prime component, such as the safety airbags. And some vehicles are stolen for a joy ride that usually ends up with the car being wrecked as part of the fun.

Making money driving a limousine requires long hours because the vehicles are hired for charges relating primarily to time used rather than distance driven. Drivers might wait at the garage several hours at a time collecting a small hourly wage only to be called for a job at the end of their shift. The job might extend the driver's day until the next morning. As such, a driver can get tired and hungry. More than one limo or luxury town car (sedan) has been snatched when the driver left the car with motor running in front of a coffee shop or hot dog stand.

The two primary periods of elevated threat for the limousine driver are during waiting periods and when a client enters or exits the vehicle. Keeping the doors locked during wait times will avoid nuisance crimes like trespassing. You'd be surprised how many times this happens. People just think it's funny to try out what it feels like to be in a limousine.

Where you go, who your clients are, and how they act can also have an effect on security. This starts with choosing carefully for whom you work. Keep in mind that fleets with better reputations often pass on or "farm out" calls from questionable clientele to smaller independent owners. Questionable clientele include people with a reputation for abusing the interior of the limousine or staying out all night. Identifying clients that rent limousines can be just as important as identifying prospective homebuyers before you take them out to show property. Credit checks are a valuable tool as well. The only time I took on a client with two first names on his license and credit cards during my experience as a driver for hire, I became suspicious and insisted that the owner guarantee the job with a cash deposit. It's a good thing I did. The credit cards turned out to be bogus.

It is not unheard of for the independent owner of a small fleet to rely heavily on referrals. Nor is it unheard of for an independent hungry for work to take on a client without a proper background check. Cash customers should be considered suspect because this helps bypass the type of background check afforded by a credit card. A ride unsecured by a credit card also means the liability is probably going to be limited to the amount of the deposit.

More often than not the types of limousines in the fleet can tell you something about the clientele you will be driving. If you see a lot of super stretched limos in unusual colors, the clientele is going to be party people and generally younger in age. For fleets that handle party people, the bulk of the hours will probably be on nights and weekends compared to limousine companies that rely primarily on corporate accounts that keep them busy during the standard five-day workweek This can be ideal if driving a limo is your second job. Just remember what the taxi drivers

The experience of working in the limousine industry can vary according to the types of cars available for hire. A service with several standard-length sedans generally service businesspeople. Vans typically run to and from the airport. Stretched specialty vehicles means the company handles parties and special events. Not only does driving a super-stretch limousine require skill and special licensing, the driver must also know how to handle people who can at times test the driver's patience.

said were their least favorite fares, young people and drunks. The presence of an onboard bar means sooner or later you will be dealing with a drunk. Aside from vandalism and having to clean up vomit, you may find yourself wrestling with a client or having to deal with a violent situation involving them. Physical injuries, lawsuits, and job termination can be the result.

Setting boundaries with clients out for an evening of fun is just as important as developing a rapport. One very good idea is to establish the itinerary at the beginning of the job when people are more serious and not vary from it as the night wears on.

Explaining that any changes or unplanned stops have to be cleared with base usually works better than just telling the customer there will be an extra charge. Of course, an extension of time will cost more anyway but people tend to go along with it until they get the bill. Rock and roll groups, especially in the 1970s and 1980s, were famous for trashing their limos with a "send me the bill" attitude, but you may very well drive less-famous clients intent on partying like rock stars that will act this way as well.

The days of celebrities needing more cameras and press are over thanks to cell phone cameras, TMZ, and social media. That's why it's the established, lower-profile garages that are typically hired by celebrities. For example, legendary diva Leontyne Price would never ride in a white limousine. She considered it beneath her, déclassé. Of course, Miss Price required the door be opened for her whenever she entered or exited the vehicle. Such service is part and parcel of traditional limousine service and changing the job from mere transport to one that takes into account security for the clientele, the vehicle, and the driver.

The protection as well as transport of clientele is really a separate, specialized profession. But whenever the driver opens his door and leaves the driver's seat, the threat level is increased. Actually, it's not much different than if you were driving your own family, especially children or the elderly. Here's a quick rundown on making a safe stop to deliver passengers:

As you approach the destination, look for a spot in front of the most direct path between the car door and the building entrance.

As you approach the destination, remind the passengers to stay seated until you open the door for them.

Always prefer a spot at curbside even if it is next to a fire hydrant or in a no parking zone.

Whether you park curbside or are forced to double-park, stop the car and spend two to three seconds checking front, back, and to the sides, ending with the left side mirror for oncoming traffic.

Roll down the window about halfway and turn off the engine. Take the keys with you as you exit. This will prevent theft and prevent you from being locked out of the car.

Double-check traffic approaching from the rear.

Look for anyone standing or approaching the vehicle as you circle the car.

Always look left, right, and finally to the rear before you open the door.

You must train yourself to comprehend and react to what you see. This means becoming more judgmental. Have an "eager" eye.

The newest way to earn a living driving is by joining Uber, which started out almost like a pizza delivery job because you drive your own car and they supply the passengers. Without the proliferation of the cell phone this type of business probably wouldn't exist. The advantage to being an Uber driver is its part-time work when you want scheduling. But pressure from established private hire transport services that are subject to regulation from state or local agencies are pressing these independent drivers to conform. Some of the regulations have to do with the cars being used, but at issue is identifying the legality and fitness of the driver. And, at the time of this writing, there is a dispute whether or not the drivers are independent contractors or employees. This affects not only benefits due the drivers but also taxation, at least indirectly. No matter how this works out, the security risk, like the status of the network itself, is still evolving.

As long as the Uber driver is allowed to operate without any visible signage, the risk of catching the eye of a robber is lower than that of a taxicab. As long as payment is electronic, the presence or exchange of cash can also minimize the threat of robbery. However, a driver in a very nice car can still be requested to a location from a third party telephone to avoid identification and carjacked. Statistics of Uber drivers being robbed are still being compiled partly because it is a relatively new way of doing business. Many Uber drivers have never worked in transportation before and indeed advertising for drivers seems to be pointed to this demographic. This inexperience could serve to increase their vulnerability.

For the Uber passengers the non-commercial appearance of the vehicle likely adds to the appeal. But not (yet) being under the licensing of a taxi and limousine commission, it is unclear just how much effort is put into background checks for Uber drivers, let alone fingerprinting and checking police or immigration records.

Preemptive Behavioral Response for the Everyday Driver

The above information should be helpful in establishing a safety protocol for anyone who is currently working or considering working in the personal transportation industry, but what about everyone else? Isn't driving so much a part of our lives that we can indeed apply many of the lessons learned by the professional?

Checklist

How to avoid being a victim of smash-and-grab or "Jugging":

Avoid making extra stops after banking or making large purchases.

If your errands include a long list of stops, prioritize so that you go directly home after visiting a bank or buying a "big ticket" item such as a computer or television set.

How to avoid being the victim of a driveway robbery:

Signaling and looking left and right are natural protocol before turning into your neighborhood.

Check the rearview mirror to see if any car turns in with you.

If you do not recognize the car behind you as you enter the neighborhood or approach your residence, keep driving.

Do not brake suddenly or do anything to acknowledge the other driver.

Leave the neighborhood as though you forgot something at the store.

If they continue to follow, dial 911 and stay on the line with the operator.

Maintain the basic safety features of your vehicle:

Make sure the remote door locking feature of your vehicle is operating.

Get in the habit of locking the doors as soon as you enter.

Do not use the switch to unlock all the doors if you are the only person exiting the vehicle.

If you door locks can be programmed:
Continue to utilize the habit of locking the doors as soon as you enter.

Program the doors to lock when the vehicle is put into gear.

Avoid programming the doors to unlock when the vehicle is put into park.

Maintain the heat and air conditioning units so that the windows do not need to be left in the open position.

Be in control of where you park:
Wherever you go, the presence of anyone that makes you feel uncomfortable in any way is justification for you to leave.

Park with the front of the vehicle facing forward.

Backing out is not only slower but more dangerous.

Backing out limits visibility of oncoming traffic as well as an approaching threat.

Always park beneath a light at night or if there is the possibility you may not be returning to the car before dark.

Park as close to the entrance of your destination as possible.

If you cannot park near your destination, try to park in view of or in line with the front door.

If you are visiting a restaurant, sit where you can see the vehicle.

Parking away from a group of cars will allow you to see around the vehicle as you approach.

Do not immediately exit the vehicle after coming to a stop.

Check the rearview, left side, and right side mirrors before opening the doors.

Do not pick up hitchhikers.

Do not open the door or open the window to speak with strangers.

Chapter 5 The Dangers of Drive-Up/ Drive-Through Services

rive-up or drive-through services include fast food restaurants, video rental machines, the Automated Teller Machine (ATM), and even dry cleaners. Perhaps the most dangerous aspect of utilizing drive-up or drive-through services can be the very distractions required by the process of placing an order or operating the necessary vending machine. But the very mindset of "quick and convenient" can promote skipping over the most basic safety concerns.

If a trip to the dry cleaners seems like the least likely scenario to be interrupted by crime, then you're probably not old enough to remember when cars could only be locked using a physical metal key. If we could turn back the clock or visit the files of nearly any newspaper (sorry, no Internet searches allowed, or for that matter no Internet), there would be plenty of stories to read containing the phrase "car stolen while owner makes a quick stop at (fill in the blank) leaving the engine running." I recently spent rush hour parked in front of my favorite dry cleaners keeping track of how many people parked by the front door and left their engine running. I also recorded how many locked their cars with a remote, locked their cars with a key or by manually engaging the door lock, or left the car unlocked with or without the windows closed. Out of twenty-one patrons, two actually went inside with the engine running, one of which was able to lock the doors just the same. Eight patrons did not lock the car doors and the remaining eleven each utilized the electronic door locks. As we have seen with the attraction to the smart phone, electronic devices

such as keyless remotes are so easy to use, the practice quickly becomes habitual. "Lock your car and take your keys" is motherly common sense but it's easy to forget what's truly at stake.

Most people think of the value of a stolen car for its resale value in whole or in parts, but the stolen vehicle is the number one getaway car for all sorts of crime. After a crime is committed with a stolen vehicle and it has been disposed of soon after, providing the police with a description and license plate number often becomes useless. Stolen vehicles are also used as "skeleton keys" or rams. Have you ever noticed the groups of nondescript posts in front of a store entrance?

Gun stores and convenience stores that contain an ATM often install barriers such as cement-filled pipes sunk as far as four feet below ground to prevent vehicles from crashing through security doors and gates. This process often leaves the vehicle wrecked and disabled, but a second vehicle is waiting for the perpetrators to make their escape.

Your personal safety is at risk but so are your passengers, including small children strapped into a car seat. If the car is abandoned while you just run inside, a smash and grab can overcome any locked doors if valuables are in reach. There is always the threat of a common robbery of money, but let's take a look at how planning or Preemptive Behavioral Response can serve to limit exposure to common threats.

The first defense is to choose the location of the business you wish to visit. It is not unusual for small modules or strip centers to contain a gasoline station

Gun stores (and for that matter convenience stores that contain an ATM) often install barriers such as cement-filled pipes sunk as far as four feet below ground to prevent vehicles from being used to ram through security doors and gates. This process often leaves the vehicle wrecked and disabled but the plan typically includes a second vehicle waiting for the perpetrators to make their escape. *Photo by the author, courtesy of Boyert Shooting Center.*

and convenience store with a dry cleaner's or fast-food restaurant either connected to or serviced by the same parking areas, exits and, entrances.

The typical convenience store is a magnet for trouble almost by design. By selling alcohol, cigarettes, snacks, and providing pay telephones and restrooms, the gasoline station/convenience store becomes a home away from home for the indigent and an ideal staging area for crime. Keep in mind that where you go dictates with whom you interact. Think of it this way: If all you want is a gallon of milk or a fresh crease in your business suit, why go to a bar? Choosing to patronize businesses more specific to your needs with no obvious connection to, or in the vicinity of, establishments that offer mood-altering drugs, legal or otherwise, will decrease your likelihood of being the victim of a crime.

Avoiding trouble during drive-up or drive-through services begins with the very same technique as when making a fuel stop. Take a lap around the parking lot and inventory of who is on the grounds. Is anyone watching you? People should be in motion at a drive-through or fast food restaurant. Anyone who is standing still should stand out.

A good example of an incident that could have been avoided by checking who was about took place in Omaha, Nebraska, in July of 2012. Video from the store parking lot distributed by Crime Stoppers shows a man sitting on the curb of the sidewalk bordering the parking spaces directly in front of the building. Five parking spaces are visible in the video clip, all of them empty. It is nighttime and we could assume that there are many parking spots to choose from. A woman drives in and parks her car in front

The distraction of using a vending machine in public can present security concerns in direct proportion to location and time of day. Any vending machine located near a drug store, liquor store, or any establishment that sells alcohol means sooner or later you're going to cross paths with someone who is inebriated or in need of drugs or drink. Vending machines that require special attention, like viewing with the aide of a curtain, could further increase risk. Note the support columns nearby that a perpetrator could hide behind in order to set up an ambush.

of the video rental machine near to where the man is seated.

As broadcast by KETV, the local ABC affiliate, anchor Rob McCartney reports that the man was "Waiting for a victim. Eventually one drives up."[1] While the woman is looking for a movie on the vending machine, the man comes up behind and says he has a gun. The man is seen walking her back to her car, maintaining close contact, and reportedly demanding all her money. After taking the money the man walks away and the woman drives off.[2]

The video from the parking lot camera was obviously edited for time because in the opening scene the parking lot is deserted except for the man. When the crime takes place, four of the five visible parking spaces are filled including the victim's car. The place of business was a drugstore so perhaps his intent could have been not only to rob someone who would be distracted by

working the vending machine but also trying his luck in obtaining prescription drugs, whichever opportunity presented itself first. Today's big drugstores are really variety stores but anyone seen leaving with a paper bag (rather than a plastic bag in which dry goods are typically dispatched) could become a target. To be on the safe side, always ask for a shopping bag to cover the telltale white paper pharmacy bag.

In this case, cash was the target even though such vending machines accept payment strictly by credit card. This would be the reason why the perpetrator was seen walking the victim back to her car. We don't actually see her open the car door because the purpose of the broadcast likely was to provide a description of the perpetrator to the public. But it seems reasonable to assume the woman had taken out her credit card to use the vending machine and left her purse in the car. Or, perhaps she had told the robber she had left her money in the car as a ruse strictly to gain time, hoping someone might intervene. Ultimately, the payment appears it may have come from her jeans pocket.

If her purse was inside the car, one has to wonder why he even bothered with approaching the woman at all once she was busy in front of the vending machine. He could have grabbed the purse and run with the same ultimate result. Maybe his original plan was to abduct the woman but something changed his mind. If the woman had pulled up while the parking area was empty rather than as busy as it appeared to be in the latter part of the video, the man could have easily taken her with him.

That the man was spending time alone in the parking lot should have been a red flag to anyone watching the cameras from inside the store. Dressed shabbily and wearing a T-shirt tied around his head would indicate his station in life, if not his state of mind. It's not worth questioning why this man was allowed to loiter, for it is our job to survive and prevail no matter what.

Thanks to movies, television, and video games it's easy to imagine the woman drawing a gun, beating the man up with karate, or choking the man out with jiu-jitsu. But once a fight starts it's rarely easy to control the outcome or predict what will happen along the way because you have no control over your opponent's thoughts or actions. Let's focus instead on our own actions and see how much we can script before last-ditch efforts and chance play a part.

The list of Preemptive Behavioral Response for a visit to the movie vending machine begins with surveillance. Who is in the parking lot? Judge any bystander like a suitor asking permission to take your daughter on her first date. A man with a white T-shirt on his head sitting on the curb rings up the following options: Come back another time or find a different vending machine. Or, call the store and tell them there is a man outside that makes you feel unsafe. If you are already out of your car when you

discover the man loitering, go directly inside the store and look for a security officer or ask for the manager. How you are treated should determine if you ever shop there again and feel free to tell them so if necessary.

The practice of circling the parking lot and looking for anyone who might do you harm should become automatic, habitual, and maybe even an art form in itself. As a result of my first training in searching for intruders whether indoors or out, the words of the instructor still ring in my ears today: "If you do not see anyone or anything out of place, look again. This time not for where they are but for where they would be hiding."

In a sense, looking for someone in the most likely hiding places is not that much different than watching for an opening to turn left across oncoming traffic, specifically at night. Initially, your eyes will pick up the headlights of each car moving in your direction. But don't let your eyes become numb in recognition to anything that is not illuminated. If all you are seeing is the headlights you will miss the one car traveling with its lights off. And that's the one that will hit you. The lights will find your eyes in periphery almost automatically. The key is to focus between the lights so the glare does not blind you. When searching space your eyes will be drawn quickly to movement just the same as they were drawn to the headlights. In the meantime, be sure to scan the entire geometry of your field of view and consciously check obvious places to hide.

In an effort to develop search habits it won't take long to develop a standard checklist of hiding places. Think of it as a collection of game pieces from a Monopoly board. Mailbox, the edges of a car body and negative space between the wheels, support column, vending machine, building corner, entry door opening with nobody going in or out indicating someone out of view was nevertheless in range of the electronic eye.

Before going further with drive-up or drive-through services, here's three simple words to remember about walk-up ATMs: don't use them. It's hard enough to generate a safe barrier when you're on line inside a vehicle, let alone stay vigilant while answering questions from a machine that is about to belch out the number-one crime magnet in the world, cash money.

As an aside, if you ever walk in to do business at a bank and the tellers are not behind a bullet-resistant barrier, leave. Some years ago, banks in Northwest Houston were victimized by one robbery after another. Word on the street was the same gang was responsible for each hit. The wave of robberies seemed to begin after several new bank branches were built to service a boom in population growth. On my first visit to the newest branch in my area, I noticed the teller windows were nothing more than open, unprotected counters. Aware of robberies that were happening more frequently in other parts of the city, I pointed this out to the bank manager. It was soon after that this very bank was robbed, along with nearly every one of the banks along the Northwest Freeway, whether they were freestanding or inside of a supermarket. Some of the robberies were violent, resulting in personal injury. Afterward, each of these banks reopened with bullet-resistant partitions. Some of the banks hired armed guards until the perpetrators were caught and the crime wave ceased.

When you're on line inside a vehicle, keep the doors locked and don't open the window until you have to. Stay far enough back from the car in front of you so that you can turn and drive out of line quickly in one motion without having to back up or make more than one turn of the wheel. The rule of thumb for guaranteeing that you are in the proper position is to make sure you can see the bottom of the rear tires of the car in front of you.

When using a drive-up ATM there are a few simple things that can be done to reduce risk, some of which are meant to limit elapsed time for the processes, i.e., exposure. Before arriving at the ATM site, remove the debit or bank card from your purse or wallet and leave it within reach. Circle the parking lot or general area and look for anyone on foot or waiting in a parked car. Approach the ATM but stop short for a moment and scan anyone moving by using the rearview and left and right side mirrors. Roll down the window when you are in front of the machine, keeping in mind that you can get closer to the machine by folding in the side-view mirror. Check the condition of the ATM by quickly scanning for dents or pry marks. Your eyes can move extremely quickly so we're not talking about much time here. If there is a sticker saying the ATM is approved for service that looks temporary or not genuine, the machine could have been tampered with and the reader may be compromised.

The moment before you put your card into the slot, inspect the interior of the slot itself. Any extra material inside the slot may indicate a pirate reader has been installed. Current machinery dictates the card is swiped and not retained so once you have worked the card through the reader you can bring it back into the vehicle. There is no need to spend time putting it back into a wallet and then putting the wallet back into a purse or shifting in the seat to stow it inside a pocket. Before pulling out make sure the driver's side window is at least more than halfway up.

Know where you are going when you pull away from the ATM window. If you have a choice of direction, such as straight ahead to a more distant exit or nearby to an exit where you will have to wait in line before turning on to a road, take the more distant exit. It is simply preferable to keep moving away from the ATM in order to put distance between yourself and anyone that might have been lying in wait nearby. This will also make it more difficult for someone to follow you without being detected.

It's not unusual for the ATM to be used for purposes other than to get cash. It's a quick, convenient way to check an account balance or make a deposit. The problem with using an ATM for services other than getting cash is that all ATM transactions appear to be the same until the conclusion. Therefore, everything that marks you as a target for robbery takes place before it is ever obvious that you are not there to make a withdrawal. The following is an example.

According to a September 9, 2015, report in *The Herald* newspaper of Rock Hill, South Carolina, a man threatened a woman at a local ATM with a gun and tried to take her money. The man was on foot wearing black clothing with his face covered when he approached the driver's side window. When the woman screamed, he told her to stop and put his hand over the return slot. But no money came out because she was there to deposit a check. The robber fired a round into the air, either for the purpose of intimidation or out of frustration, as he ran to a getaway car waiting nearby.[3]

Now let's analyze how the event could have escalated and how it could have been avoided. Personally, I don't trust an ATM to accept and properly record a deposit. I like to have face-to-face verification as well as a receipt. Maybe the woman was in too much of a rush to get out of her car or just used to doing everything electronically. That the incident took place at about 8:30 p.m., long after the bank had closed and she was comfortable with an automated transaction, may support the latter. But if the woman had only taken the extra time to go inside the bank during normal business hours, she likely would not have been a victim. His MO was to watch for someone to drive up to the ATM and by the report not pull in tight against the machine. Remember, he was able to reach in and cover the return slot with his hand.

We also learned that a getaway car was waiting. This means the woman did not circle the building and look for a parked car with someone inside. Ultimately, the woman was very lucky because it appears that cash was the robber's only goal. That he was armed and may have had an accomplice in the getaway car leaves open the possibility the woman could have been kidnapped, threatened, or even tortured to give up her personal identification number (PIN), allowing the robber to access her account. Her vehicle could have been used for additional crimes or profit from its sale and worst of all, the woman could have been killed or sold into slavery.

If the vulnerability inherent in using drive-up or drive-through services seems overwhelming, the fact is that this is nothing new. It's just that we've come to rely on outside help to provide our own security and a modern vehicle transmitting relatively little road noise could draw just about anyone into a false sense of security. Consider the efficiency provided by the cars we drive. If we did not have electronic door locks, each individual door would have to be locked manually. A habit of checking the latch visually would quickly develop. The inconvenience of a lone driver having to get out and crank up a rear window might also make us more aware. A reaction such as "Damn it, I went to the trouble of stopping halfway down the driveway to get out and go around to the rear passenger side window just to crank it up and make sure the button was down," just might make us more determined to watch out for our own safety.

A recent book signing for *The Shooter's Bible Guide to Home Defense* morphed into a "town hall" meeting of sorts at which I answered questions about specific safety concerns. One young couple ran a business servicing vending machines all over the city of Houston. Their primary concern was being robbed when they were collecting from the coin boxes. If you think operating a vending machine is distracting, imagine the attention it takes to open the machine, restock it, and reset the internal workings. The first answer is to provide a second (or third) set of eyes.

Consider the origin of the phrase, "riding shotgun." When horse-drawn carriage was the primary mode of transportation, standard practice was for the driver to control a team of horses. The attention and physical labor involved in motivating and steering as many as ten horses over rough ground left little opportunity for scanning the surroundings for trouble, let alone handling a weapon. Security was the primary job of the man sitting next to him armed with a rifle, handgun, or shotgun. The shotgun was the preferred force multiplier because its scatter of "shot" made up for accuracy that was lacking in most guns of the day. It is important to remember, this was the time before the science of reactive bullets, such as hollow points that expand, acting to increase the wound canal and speeding up the elapsed time before bleed out. Even a weapon with as many as six shots available before reloading might not be capable of providing the same amount of "ventilation" as a shotgun.

Riding shotgun in today's world need not be as obvious as hiring a cowboy with a shotgun on his lap. Simply having someone else with you decreases your odds of being targeted, especially if each party is acting in a vigilant manner. If your partner is texting or talking on the phone they might as well not be there. If one of you have a cell phone and at least appear to be videotaping your trip to the vending machine, that might also serve as a deterrent. Be aware that if one or both of you are armed you still need to offer the body language of being vigilant.

I recently witnessed a woman holding her small dog while accessing a DVD vending machine located outside of a drugstore. The little yapper may or may not have been capable of a meaningful bite but its barking would at least alert the woman when to run. In addition, allow me to point out one other aspect of the surveillance video from the robbery of the woman at the movie vending machine in the drugstore parking lot. The perpetrator's actions and body language was extremely low-key as he approached the woman and convinced her to move back to her car, reportedly under threat of being shot. Making it look as though he knew his victim and was simply walking her back to her car was a necessity in order for him to pull off the robbery without attracting attention. I doubt the perpetrator in this case would have chosen the woman with the little dog in her arms for precisely this reason.

Preemptive Behavioral Response for Drive-Up/Drive-Through Services

Checklist

Consider the location of the stores and banks that you frequent.

Ask yourself:
Does it also sell liquor or cigarettes?
Is it adjacent to a business that sells liquor or cigarettes?

Drive through the parking area and take notice of who is in attendance.

Ask yourself:
Is anyone waiting around for no apparent reason?
Is anyone in the area dressed inappropriately, such as covering their face or wearing heavy clothes on a warm day, sunglasses on a cloudy day, etc.?
Is there a car parked nearby with a driver inside waiting for no apparent reason?
What structures could be used to hide behind?

If you were playing hide and seek where would you hide?

When you park your car turn off the engine, lock the doors, and take your keys.

Do not leave a child unattended in the car.

When on line for service from inside your car, stay far enough behind the car in front of you so that you can see the rear wheels. This will allow you to maneuver out of line.

At the Bank

Do not use an ATM for making a deposit or checking a balance.

No matter your purpose or intention, in the eyes of a criminal your presence at the ATM will always signal a cash withdrawal.

When visiting a bank lobby:

Are the tellers behind bullet-resistant glass?

If not, the bank is more attractive to robbery than other banks that are more secure.

Do not use a walk-up ATM.

Before driving up to an ATM, circle the facility and look for anyone that is on foot or waiting inside a parked car.

If you are in line for the ATM, stay back from the car in front of you so that you can maneuver quickly out of line.

Have your card out and ready before reaching the ATM.

Pull in the side mirror so you can get as close as possible to the slots and keypad without damaging your car.

Look around.

Leaving your car in gear with a foot on the brake is a double-edged sword. If there are pedestrians in the area, leaving in a panic may result in hitting an innocent passerby.

Check the condition of the ATM. If it looks roughed up, a pirate card reader may have been installed.

Whenever you are in line, even waiting at a stoplight, maintain enough distance from the car in front of you so that you can turn and drive out of line quickly to escape trouble without having to back up or make more than one turn of the wheel. A rule of thumb is to make sure you can see some portion of the rear tires of the vehicle in front of you.

If there is an inspection sticker that is too obvious or does not appear genuine, a pirate card reader may have been installed.

If the transaction does not go through for any reason, check your balance as soon as possible to see if your data has been compromised.

After you swipe your card, place it inside the car but do not take the time or attention to return it to your wallet or purse at this time.

Look around.

It's natural to want to count the money dispensed by the machines but an ATM, especially one connected directly to a bank, is highly accurate and regulated. In the event of any irregularity, the only people that can help are inside the bank or on the telephone so drive off as soon as you have the money and/or receipt in your hands.

Drive off in a direction that offers the least resistance. Choose a path that keeps you moving and allows you to exit to the street quickly.

If you are picking up a prescription at a drugstore that also sells all manner of dry goods, make sure to ask for a bag used for general merchandise.

A white paper bag typically used to hold prescription drugs can attract the wrong attention.

If you are going to use a vending machine located on the exterior of a business exposed to the parking lot, choose only the busier hours to do so. No one should be standing or sitting around waiting.

Take someone with you to watch your back while you manipulate the machine and make your choices.

Remain vigilant and demonstrate body language bordering on arrogance that indicates awareness of your surroundings.

Chapter 6 How Safety Plays a Part in Choosing a Handgun for Personal Defense

In comparison to martial arts, edged weapons, Tasers, and chemical sprays, the firearm offers the greatest opportunity to survive an attack. One reason why the firearm is the superior defensive weapon is due to its ability to project force. The projection of force allows victims that are lesser in terms of size, strength, or numbers to prevent a superior fighting force from making actual physical contact. Just as a single anti-personnel rocket can destroy a platoon of enemy soldiers from afar, even frail elderly people with adequate handgun skills can defeat one or more large men that mean them harm. While carrying a handgun for personal defense is sound preparation, it nevertheless burdens the operator with a considerable level of responsibility. For this reason, the ability to handle your firearm safely should play a part in how you choose a handgun for personal defense.

The space devoted to choosing a firearm in my second book, the *Shooter's Bible Guide to Home Defense*, offers insights into all types of shotguns, rifles, and handguns but ultimately recommends high capacity weapons with the weight and ergonomics to make them controllable and comfortable to shoot. However, the firearm chosen for personal defense may be very different from the guns kept around the house. For example, firearms portable enough to be carried on a regular basis, most often concealed, are necessarily smaller, so a compromise in size and capacity is to be expected.

The first method or approach to choosing a firearm for personal defense that I would suggest is based on ergonomics, a word bandied about in gun publications all the time. What it means to you is how well the gun fits your individual hands. If the gun feels clumsy in your hands, it's going to be difficult to control and ultimately destroy your confidence. If you are lucky you will never have to fire a gun in anger but what about the hundreds of times per year you will handle the gun taking it from your nightstand and putting it into a holster or purse? Obviously, being clumsy is not safe.

The second part of this approach to choosing a firearm further explores ergonomics and explains how the physical relationship between your hand and the trigger directly affects accuracy. The third part of the study introduces new drills to help you become a more accurate shooter in less-than-favorable conditions. It is important to remember if you cannot hit the target you will not be able to stop a threat and you could be endangering others in the process.

Accepting the Personal Defense Handgun into Your Lifestyle

Choosing firearms for personal defense means that each gun you employ must function within a very specific context. That context is your lifestyle as defined by the actions and limitations of your daily routine, especially when you're in public. We've already spoken in previous chapters about how preemptive behavioral response are preparatory behaviors that provide layers of protection. Certainly carrying a firearm for personal defense does have the potential to present a formidable barrier, especially if the operator is well-trained and maintains their ability with at least a minimum amount of practice. But for any form of preparation to remain effective it must be used habitually. However, before any action or practice can become a habit, the actor must find it agreeable and accept it physically.

What does it mean for an action or a practice to be agreeable and accepted physically? The agreement to perform the action may require a compromise such as "my purse is a little heavier but not enough to dissuade me from carrying my gun." Ultimately, the necessity of performing a physical action must be accepted without complaint. In the case of choosing a firearm for personal defense, having a gun with you should not be frustrating, painful, or prevent you from doing whatever chores are necessary in your daily life.

The Evolution of Today's Carry Gun, A Brief Perspective

There is an old saying that goes something like, "Is that gun comfortable or is it comforting?" The inquisitor is actually saying, "That's a mighty big gun you got there. It must be a pain to carry but I bet it makes you feel safe." The reason that's an "old" saying is the choice in handguns used to be limited to either a big steel-framed revolver or a full size Browning 1911 Government model like your dad or granddad might have brought home from World War II.

The 1911 Anniversary edition from Cylinder and Slide is a perfect example of the full-size Browning 1911 Government .45. Weighing in at about 40 ounces unloaded, it was never meant for concealment. It's taken quite a bit of technology to produce smaller guns that are lighter in weight and function reliably. *Photo courtesy of Cylinder and Slide.*

When loaded, either of these types of guns could weigh as much as three pounds. The development of smaller and lighter handguns didn't really pick up speed until the 1990s after Gaston Glock introduced the polymer-framed handgun to the American public. However, the Glock GL17, so named for its seventeen-round capacity magazine, was still the size of a police service pistol designed to be carried in a duty holster worn without concern for concealment or convenient portability.

In the war between "plastic"-framed handguns and metallic-framed handguns, American makers fought back with the development of space age alloys such as titanium and scandium as well as improvements in aluminum composition. Metal-framed guns were getting lighter and easier to carry but the use of "space age" materials made them more expensive to produce than their steel counterparts, let alone the Glock 17 that could easily be mass-produced. With more states issuing concealed carry permits, all the makers, including Glock, discovered that guns could be made lighter and easier to carry simply by making them smaller.

While many of the first compact and subcompact semiautomatic pistols were prone to malfunction, smaller revolvers remained reliable. Given that cycling a double-action revolver is strictly a manual process powered directly by the operator, downsizing revolvers to about the size of a six-inch long by four-inch tall index card has had no effect on reliability. The only side effect was reduced capacity, as five-round cylinders became the standard for centerfire calibers. But for semiautomatic pistols, wherein the motion of the reciprocating slide was responsible for both loading the chamber and evacuating the emptied case, reducing the length and the weight of the slide presented a challenge to reliability. The shorter, faster-moving slide offered less time and opportunity to strip a round from the magazine and move it cleanly into the chamber. The change in timing played havoc

with nearly every aspect of the design. For example, the magazine spring had to move the rounds upward more efficiently. And the recoil spring that tempers slide velocity as well as the amount of force with which the action returned to battery became all the more critical. While these engineering challenges were being dealt with, the question of capacity became an issue. Consumers wondered (and argued) over whether they should carry larger calibers such as .45 ACP that limited space in the magazine or choose a gun chambered for smaller diameter rounds such as 9mm in order to boost capacity.

The current field of concealable handguns now offers a wide variety of designs as well as calibers. Reliability issues in today's smaller semiautomatic pistols are all but nonexistent. Lightweight materials and the mating of polymer and steel subframes make the guns lighter and stronger than ever. When I began my career as a firearms-test professional, frame breakage and cycling failures due to poor fit was a regular occurrence. Malfunctions occur so rarely during evaluations currently being performed that higher overall ratings per weapon are almost entirely based on performance rather than function versus failure. Much of the credit should go to advancements not only in metallurgy, polymers, and injection molding techniques, but the use of computer numerically controlled (CNC) machinery. Today you can get almost any size handgun in a variety of calibers and there is greater variation in how the different types of guns are to be operated than ever before. The current trend is to make the guns thinner and more concealable as the evolution of the handgun continues at a remarkable pace.

Choosing a Handgun Based on Safe Handling Practices

If the above makes choosing a handgun for personal defense more difficult, then I would suggest

Today you can get almost any size handgun in a variety of calibers and there is greater variation in how the different types of guns operate than ever before. The XD series from Springfield Armory is a good example. Available in multiple calibers the (left to right) XDM 5.5, XDM 3.8, and the XD Mod 2 all operate with the same firing mechanism with little if any difference in handling characteristics. The XDM 5.5 was designed as a target pistol, the Mod 2 for deeper concealment, and the XDM 3.8 is versatile enough to fit any role in between. By choosing guns that operate the same way, the owner can respond with the same muscle memory no matter the situation.

narrowing the field based on how comfortable you would be performing the actions necessary to ensure safe handling of the weapon in a variety of circumstances. Not just at a shooting range but in more challenging circumstances, such as seated behind the steering wheel of a car or even when adjusting your clothing to use a restroom. Imagine being so comfortable with a handgun that picking it up and stowing it in your favorite carry system (holster, purse, etc.) would be as natural as putting on a watch or a ring. Based on the following review of how each design affects safe handling protocol, ask yourself which type of gun would best fit the mode of carry you use most often and your individual level of strength and hand-eye coordination.

Safe Handling Practices for Revolvers

Revolvers have the great advantage of not requiring the power of the ammunition to cycle the gun. This means you can leave it loaded without the fear of a magazine spring being weakened beneath the weight of the rounds piled on top of it.

The downside of revolver carry is that of limited capacity, although some models, though bulky, hold as many as eight rounds of 9mm, .357 Magnum, .38 Special, or .38 Super. Other revolvers currently in production are chambered for .45 Long Colt, .45 ACP, .44 Special, and .44 Magnum.

In terms of safe handling, the double-action revolver is probably the safest of all handguns. What we always seek to avoid is the hammer dropping unintentionally

Before the successful downsizing of semiautomatic pistols, the only option for carrying a handgun offering more than five or six rounds was a large bulky revolver weighing about 40 ounces. Today you can get seven and even eight round revolvers, but the sheer size of such guns makes them unwieldy. It's much easier to blend a smaller pistol capable of holding eight or more rounds into your lifestyle.

on the firing pin and transferring energy to the primer, setting off a round. In order for the hammer of a double-action revolver to cause ignition it must first travel rearward like a fighter winding up to throw a punch. Not only does pressing the trigger of a double-action revolver retract the hammer until it breaks free to strike the firing pin, it also rotates the cylinder to provide access to a fresh round, hence the name double-action.

One of the biggest dangers in operating any firearm is to have a piece of cloth, such as a shirttail, snag on to the trigger as the gun is holstered. A stock, double-action trigger (as delivered from the factory) usually offers about 10 to 12 pounds of resistance so an unintentional discharge in this manner is not likely unless the trigger has been greatly modified to lower resistance. In the event that the trigger is moved accidentally, the cylinder will, as previously mentioned,

rotate simultaneously as the hammer moves to the rear. Therefore, holding the trigger finger against the cylinder will allow you to monitor interference with the trigger.

Another possibility that can lead to an unintentional fire is if the hammer itself is accidentally moved rearward. This could happen should the hammer spur snag against a surface, such as the interior of a fanny pack or the zipper at the mouth of a concealment purse that is not completely open. Revolvers of modern design will not allow the firing pin to strike the primer unless the trigger is pressed.

Holding the thumb atop the hammer spur will eliminate this problem altogether. Single-action revolvers are rarely used for concealed carry anymore, but keeping the thumb atop the hammer in down position is critical for safe handling. If you should choose a revolver with a reduced hammer spur or a

Modern double-action revolvers are capable of firing with a very light trigger when the hammer is pulled back manually by the operator. That's why it's important to always handle (and carry) a "DA" revolver with the hammer down. Placing the thumb behind the hammer during administrative handling ensures safety.

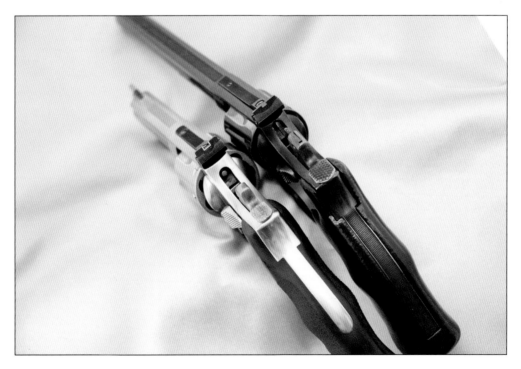

Modern revolvers have been made safer to carry by the application of a transfer bar. The gun on the right has the firing pin mounted directly on the hammer. Though not as likely as in single action revolvers of traditional design, the possibility of the hammer spur being accidentally struck with sufficient force to strike the primer of the round positioned beneath it and set off a shot still nevertheless exists. The more recent model revolver on the left was constructed with a transfer bar that rises into position only when the trigger is pressed. It is the transfer bar that completes the connection between the face of the hammer and the firing pin by command of the trigger only.

The double-action-only revolver, like this Smith & Wesson 340 PD, is a great concealment weapon because it is ultra-lightweight and its profile is unspoiled by the jagged edge of an exposed hammer. But without a hammer spur beneath the operator's thumb, how is the best way to ensure safe handling? The answer is to place the trigger finger in contact with the cylinder. Should anything snag the trigger, the operator will be alerted by rotation of the cylinder.

revolver that operates with a shrouded or an enclosed hammer such as the Smith & Wesson Centennial series "J-frame" revolvers, handling the gun with the trigger finger against the cylinder is mandatory.

Safe Handling Practices for the Double-Action-Only Semiautomatic Pistol

Double-action semiautomatic pistols that use a falling hammer for ignition are also very safe handguns by design. The hammer moves rearward towards its release point in direct proportion to how far the trigger is pressed. As with a double-action revolver, handling a double-action semiauto with the thumb atop the hammer is a necessity. The gun is simply not going to go off unless the hammer is first moved to the rear.

Safe Handling Practices for the Traditional Double-Action Semiautomatic Pistol

A variation of the double-action semiautomatic pistol is often referred to as Traditional Double-Action or TDA. In this design, the gun can be handled safely with the hammer in the down position. A blocking device prevents the hammer face from being driven forward with enough force to strike the firing pin. A second block to prevent the firing pin from moving is also commonly found in this design. However, after the first shot rearward movement of the slide leaves the hammer back, just a small increment from the point at which it is set to release toward the firing pin. In this condition the only function of the trigger is to release the hammer. Therefore, it is referred to as being in single-action mode. In single-action mode, the amount of force it

Safe administrative handling of the double-action, or in this case double/single-action, semiautomatic pistol requires holding the thumb down against the hammer.

takes to press the trigger and the distance the trigger must travel before releasing a shot is greatly reduced.

The intention of the TDA design is to provide two distinct advantages. The first shot does not require the operation of a secondary action such as deactivating a safety lever. The second shot and each one thereafter can then be released with a superior action that requires less motion, presents less resistance, and therefore offers greater precision. Holstering a TDA pistol in single-action mode, or for that matter simply moving it from a tabletop to a nightstand drawer with the hammer back, is unsafe. The recommended course of action is to return the pistol to double-action mode by pressing the

mechanical decocker lever located either on the frame or on the slide itself, depending on the design. The CZ and Sig Sauer pistols offer frame-mounted decocking levers. Beretta M9 type pistols have their decocking levers mounted on the slide.

Be aware that TDA pistols will enter single-action mode not just after firing but also upon the act of loading the weapon. While most TDA pistols do indeed have a mechanical decocker that is very easy to use, there are still a few models that require the operator to lower the hammer manually.

Traditional double-action pistols without a mechanical decocker require more skill to handle safely or at

The decocking lever of a double/single-action pistol such as the Sig Sauer P229 allows the gun to be transitioned from hammer back, single-action mode to a safe hammer down position without having to touch the trigger or the hammer.

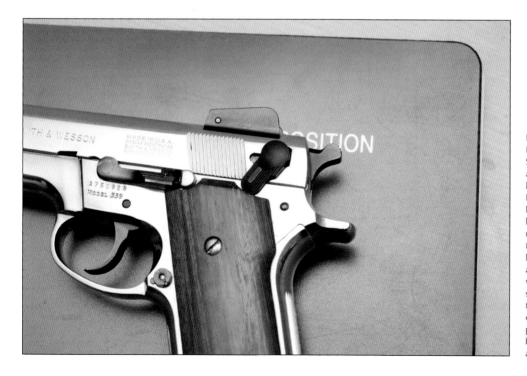

Like many of the 92 series Beretta pistols, this older Smith & Wesson features a decocking and safety lever mounted on the slide. Depressing the decocker lever safely drops the hammer without additional manipulation and can also function as a safety. The lever is shown pointing at approximately 7 o'clock which deactivates the firing system completely. Moving the lever back to horizontal or the 9 o'clock position prepares the first shot to be fired using the double-action mode.

least greater patience. Manually lowering the hammer means holding the hammer back while pressing the trigger until you hear it release. Certainly there are more than a few pitfalls here. Suppose your hands are wet or the hammer is slick with oil? Thankfully, guns that require the hammer to be reset manually to the double-action position also have thumb safeties that lock the hammer in place. Being patient enough to activate the safety and waiting until you have a safe backstop at which to point the muzzle while you decock manually is likely the better way to proceed.

In the case of both the traditional double-action and the double-action-only pistols, it is necessary to cover the hammer with the strong hand thumb to not only monitor interference with the trigger but also to prevent the slide from moving. This is because there is no mechanism to lock the slide in place. It is not unusual for friction between the slide and the interior of a holster to cause the slide to shift rearward out of position. If the slide is then moved far enough to the point of being out of battery (with the mouth of the chamber no longer sealed against the breech), the round in the chamber may be left grossly out of position or ejected altogether.

Think of how dangerous this could be if this should occur while you were at home. In any event, the gun would have to be reloaded.

Any pistol that does not offer a safety that locks the slide in battery (the closed position) is in danger of being rendered useless. Reholstering in a tight space can present enough friction to move the slide rearward and dislodge a chambered round. That's why holding the thumb behind the slide is a good idea.

Safe Handling Practices for the Browning 1911 Pistol

The Browning 1911 design is among the safest handgun actions of all to handle, both administratively and during an actual shooting sequence, because its design includes a user-operated mechanical safety. Once the slide of a 1911 has been moved rearward so that the chamber can be filled, the hammer remains in the rearward position ready to strike. It is the responsibility of the operator to then activate the frame-mounted thumb safety. The thumb safety rotates into position, not only seizing the hammer, but also locking the slide in the forward (closed) position. By activating the thumb safety it is not necessary to place the thumb atop the hammer spur to monitor unintended contact with the trigger or prevent the slide from moving out of battery. Instead, the operator places the strong hand thumb beneath the safety lever, applying upward pressure to make sure it remains activated in the "on-safe" position.

With the gun on "safe" there is no danger of the slide being forced out of battery due to friction against the mouth of a holster or other incidental contact.

Detractors of the 1911 system point to the trigger, which slides only a short distance to the break. In my view, this makes the trigger easier to manipulate without pushing the sights off center. Since hitting the intended target is the best insurance against collateral damage, one might consider this to be a safety

The thumb-operated safety of the Browning 1911 design functions as a veritable on/off switch. Holding the 1911 with the thumb pressing upwards from beneath to lock it into the safety-on position makes this pistol extremely safe to handle despite the appearance of the hammer in its rearward position.

feature in itself. However, the primary objection from those inexperienced with this design pertains to the appearance of the hammer jutting out from the rear of the weapon when the action is cocked. This seems to make some people uncomfortable, as if the hammer is likely to fall suddenly like a door slamming shut due to a sudden breeze. Perhaps the appearance of the hammer creates a subliminal effect expressed as fear that some process has been left incomplete or that the gun is broken and whatever is holding the hammer back will let go at any moment. But the 1911 design should not be confused with the single-action revolver of days gone by. Most of today's guns include a firing pin block that makes it impossible for the gun to go off unless the finger is pressing the trigger. Albeit it is the responsibility of the operator to activate the safety, the important distinction between the single-action revolver or any other design is that the 1911's thumb-operated safety provides a veritable on/off switch.

Safe Handling Practices for the Striker-Fired Semiautomatic Pistol

With all the emphasis placed on controlling the hammer, the most popular semiautomatic pistols being sold today utilize a striker rather than a hammer and firing pin to ignite the ammunition. If the hammer and firing pin mechanism can be compared to a hammer and chisel, the striker could be illustrated by the mechanics of taking a shot in a game of pool. If the muscles and tendons within the arm are in a sense spring-loaded, the pool cue can be seen as the striker with the cue ball imagined as the surface of the primer. What this means in terms of safe handling is that there is no hammer or other mechanism of ignition visible to the operator. Should any foreign object make contact with the trigger strong enough to press it rearward, there will be no prior warning. There are other safeguards in play, however.

The face or contact surface of the trigger found on most striker-fired pistols are hinged or have a secondary lever that is centrally located away from the edges. This helps avoid foreign objects from being able to press the trigger fully to the rear. A few striker-fired semiautos also provide a thumb-operated safety that will in effect "turn off" the firing mechanism but does not prevent the slide from moving should it meet enough resistance while holstering. The Springfield Armory XD and XDM series pistols go one step further by adding a grip-pressure-operated safety. The trigger cannot be activated unless the web of the hand has fully compressed the grip safety located at the upper edge along the rear of the grip.

The primary rule of firearms safety is never place your finger on the trigger until the sights are on a target you are willing to destroy. In lieu of whatever other safety mechanisms are offered by a given firearm, keeping your finger outside the trigger guard will prevent an unintentional discharge. Safe handling of a striker-fired pistol requires a very specific hand position to ensure safety. Here is what it looks like:

Have you ever seen anyone replicate the form of a gun with his or her hands? When we were kids we stuck out our index finger as if it were the barrel, closed our remaining fingers to illustrate the body of the grip and extended our thumbs upwards as if it were the hammer, much like a single-action revolver or "cowboy" gun.

Applying this same position to the handgun can keep us safe. Holding the grip of our gun with the lower three fingers and keeping the index finger alongside of the frame keeps it outside the trigger guard. The thumb is placed directly upon the back of the slide to prevent it from coming out of battery. This somewhat-open grip is especially effective should the gun offer a grip safety. For example, holding a Springfield Armory XD or XDM pistol in this manner provides even greater security by not compressing the grip safety, creating a bridge over the upper portion of the grip preventing the action from moving to fire.

Children have been sent home from school for mimicking a handgun but it's really the beginning of good safety habits. The finger is held straight and outside the trigger guard.

The Springfield Armory XD and XDM series pistols offer an added safety feature that comes into play when the thumb is held behind the slide. Borrowing from the 1911 design, the XD/XDM series grip safety must be compressed in order for the firing mechanism to work. Accessories such as the LaserMax Micro II pulsating laser attached to the rails of the Mod 2 can be invaluable in any confrontation.

Bullet Points

Handgun Ergonomics Review

In choosing a handgun for personal defense ask yourself, "How easily would it be to internalize each of the following techniques to the point at which I could perform them as automatically as I can button a shirt or tie my shoes?"

Hand Positions for Safe Handling as per Design

Single-Action Revolver

Index finger of strong hand outside the trigger guard.

Strong hand thumb resting atop the hammer spur with hammer down.

Note: hammer in down position over a loaded chamber ONLY if the revolver is equipped with a firing pin safety, or transfer bar safety.

Never holster or otherwise carry a single-action revolver with the hammer back.

Double-Action Revolver

Index finger of strong hand outside the trigger guard riding against the exterior of the cylinder.

Strong hand thumb resting atop the hammer spur with hammer down.

Note: older models of double-action revolver that feature a "nose pin" (firing pin mounted directly on the hammer) should not be carried with a loaded chamber beneath the hammer.

Never holster or otherwise carry a double-action revolver with the hammer back.

If the double-action revolver operates with its hammer not visible but enclosed by the frame (sometimes called "hammerless"), be sure to ride the index finger alongside the exterior of the cylinder.

If the hammer is shrouded, place the strong hand thumb on the small but exposed portion of the hammer spur.

If the hammer spur has been reduced or removed altogether, place the strong hand thumb on the outer contour of hammer or the remnant of the hammer spur.

Double-Action Only and Traditional Double-Action (TDA) Semiautomatic Pistols

Index finger of strong hand outside the trigger guard, preferably above the trigger guard and alongside the frame.

Strong hand thumb resting atop the hammer spur with hammer down.

Monitor any movement of the hammer and slide.

Never holster or otherwise carry a TDA pistol with the hammer back unless a mechanical safety is applied.

If the gun is equipped with a mechanical decocker always use it to lower the hammer before holstering or whenever the sights of the gun are off target.

If a gun requires manual decocking from single-action mode and does not have a working mechanical safety, this is a poor choice of weaponry in my opinion and should be disposed of.

If a gun requires manual decocking from single-action mode and does have a working manual safety, put the gun on safe at the conclusion of fire. Move to a position where a fired round will be safely blocked and absorbed without ricochet before attempting to lower the hammer manually.

Browning 1911 Action Semiautomatic Pistol

Index finger of strong hand outside the trigger guard, preferably above the trigger guard and alongside the frame.

Strong hand thumb rides beneath the platform of the thumb safety.

Upward pressure is applied to the underside of the thumb safety to prevent it from rotating downward to "off-safe" ready to fire.

Striker-Fired Semiautomatic Pistol

Index finger of strong hand outside the trigger guard, preferably above the trigger guard and alongside the frame.

Strong hand thumb resting atop the back of the slide.

Monitor for movement of the slide.

Chapter 7 Handgun Accuracy as a Component of Safety

hile conducting a search for safety rules for handling firearms, I was surprised that none of them led off with "treat all guns as if they are loaded" and "never point a gun at something you are not willing to destroy." Nor did I see instructions to keep your finger off the trigger until you have the sights on a target that has been identified as a threat, but that would be to paraphrase the original code. However, the NRA website does offer these tips:

1. Always keep the gun pointed in a safe direction.
2. Always keep your finger off the trigger until ready to shoot.
3. Always keep the gun unloaded until ready for use.

The instructions then change format from numerated priorities to "bullet points" beginning with "When using or storing a gun, always follow these NRA rules: The first rule listed reads, 'Know your target and what is beyond.'"[1]

Up until now we have concentrated on recommendations for the safe handling of firearms not necessarily during live fire practice at the range, but rather during administrative handling. But what about safety during an actual firefight? Knowing your target and what is beyond should be of the highest priority.

Every Bullet Strikes Something

The only justification to draw and fire is to prevent the death or bodily harm of yourself or someone else.

If you are not striking your intended target, you are not doing an effective job of stopping the threat. And no matter your intention, every bullet is going to strike something. Therefore, accuracy is in itself a safety rule.

The fundamentals of accurate shooting, stance, grip, sight alignment, and trigger control are well known. The purpose of the following is to enhance the student's ability to master these fundamentals.

The most important thing to know about achieving accuracy with a firearm or in this case a handgun is that no matter what comes before, make sure the sights are aligned when the gun goes off. As much practice as this can require, there is one important physical factor that can help the shooter reach this goal much sooner. It has to do with how the hand, and therefore the index finger, lines up with the trigger.

We have already recommended choosing a handgun for personal defense based on individual dexterity strictly in relation to safe handling procedures. Instructions for specific safe handling methods have been delineated based on the physical characteristics of each type of gun determined by their different operational systems. The reader was advised to choose the type of handgun to which they could most easily apply the recommended hand position in order to produce the greatest margin of safety during administrative handling. Let's say you chose a pistol operating with the traditional double-action design. There are many such "TDA" pistols on the market but which one is best for you? Again this is a choice based on individual dexterity. This time we're looking for how the gun fits your hand so that you can work the trigger with the greatest amount of control.

In my view, trigger control means the ability to move the trigger to the point of ignition with the least amount of disruption to the perfect sight picture. (Meaning front sight level with the rear sight and centered within the rear sight notch.) The only way to achieve this no matter what the firing system is to press the trigger rearward in a straight line. But here is the problem. The way our fingers are constructed, hinged via a series of joints, the tip of the finger is unable to move directly rearward when we close our hands. Instead, our fingers curl, resulting in our index finger describing an arc rather than a straight line.

As a result, the shooter must fight to maintain sight alignment throughout the duration of the press.

One method of reducing the curvature of the line drawn by the index finger as it presses rearward is to raise the hand on the grip.

The higher the hand is placed on the pistol grip, the more the index finger tends to drop down on to the face of the trigger. This helps isolate the pad of the index finger as the key point in contact with the trigger. Mechanically, this all but removes flexing of the joint located just below the fingertip, reducing curl. With movement now hinged primarily from the larger second joint, the result is a more direct path with less inherent deflection to sight alignment.

A high grip also offers the benefit of applying more strength to counteract muzzle flip. That's why competitive

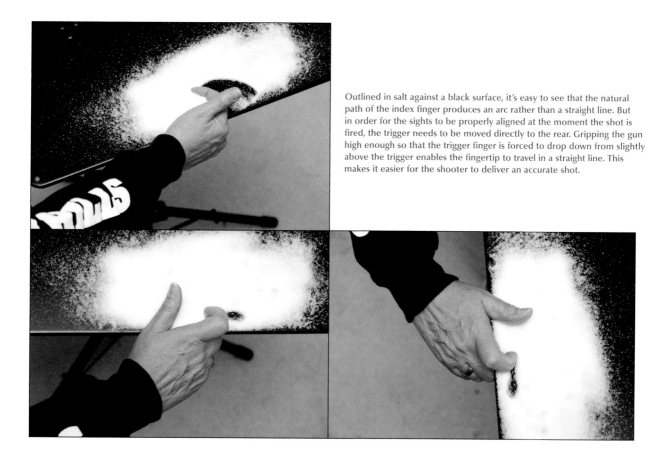

Outlined in salt against a black surface, it's easy to see that the natural path of the index finger produces an arc rather than a straight line. But in order for the sights to be properly aligned at the moment the shot is fired, the trigger needs to be moved directly to the rear. Gripping the gun high enough so that the trigger finger is forced to drop down from slightly above the trigger enables the fingertip to travel in a straight line. This makes it easier for the shooter to deliver an accurate shot.

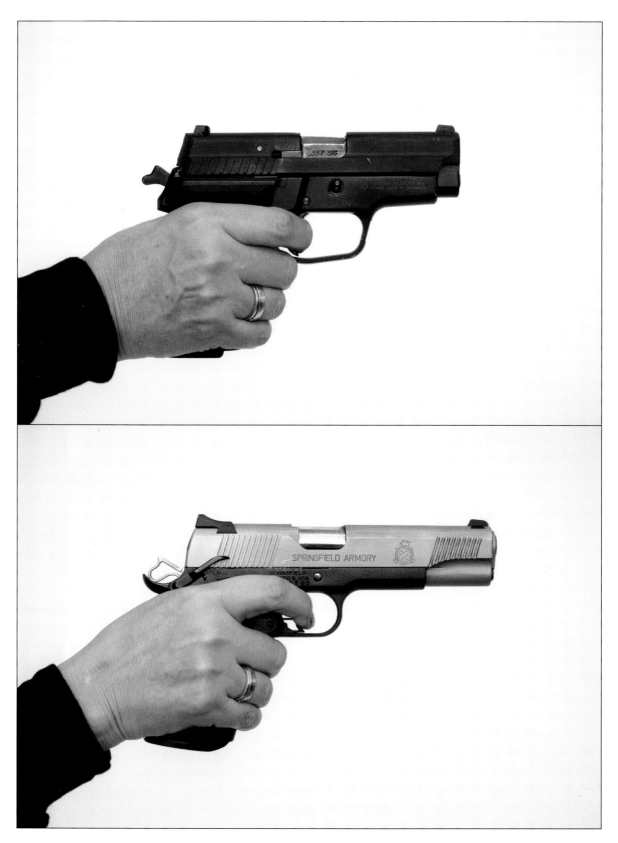

Due to the physical mechanics of the human finger, choosing a pistol that offers a higher grip can make it easier to press the trigger in a straight line. This gives the shooter a better chance of hitting their intended target and stopping the threat.

shooters prefer using a "high hold" and a gun with less vertical distance between the top of the grip and the center of the barrel, a measurement commonly referred to as "hand to bore axis." Muzzle flip is the upward movement of the pistol in reaction to recoil produced by each shot. The sooner muzzle flip is concluded, the sooner the gun can be pointed at the target and fired effectively. This means elapsed time between multiple shots can be reduced.

As a result, the second way that individual dexterity can help you choose a gun for personal defense is by determining which handgun offers your hand the highest position on the grip.

Improve Accuracy by Sharpening Instincts

It's easy to track the sights and respond by steering the front sight to the center of the rear sight notch until the gun goes off when you're shooting on a bright sunny day. But most assaults do not happen in brightly-lit conditions for several reasons. Most crimes occur under the cover of at least partial darkness simply because criminals know that darkness makes it more difficult for victims to see them coming and for witnesses to get a good look at them. Have you ever heard of anyone slipping away into the daylight? We could add that as the day goes on people in need of drugs become more desperate to purchase a supply. As the day's drinking adds up, alcohol-driven abuse is also more likely to come into play.

For anyone preparing to defend with a handgun, the ability to take aim is a precious skill readily taxed by a reduction in ambient light. There are many innovations to assist handgunners in "low light," including night sights that glow, lights that attach to the pistol, flashlights that are small enough they can be integrated with one's shooting grip, and laser systems that project the desired point of impact. I would recommend training with any or all of these accessories. But what about the human component paired with the handgun? All we have is our eyes and the ability to perceive. In a sense

our eyes are machines that need to be maintained, not unlike the gun or the accessories mentioned above. But perception is more fluid. It is at least partially a result of experience. For example, my vision is not really sharp enough to read most street signs at a distance beyond say, thirty-five yards. But if I know the name of the street I am looking for I can find it before the individual letters are clear. Here is one example of how. We were traveling in a car and looking to turn right onto a street named Western Rosharon. I say, "There it is" to the amazement of my companions when the sign has barely come into view. How did I know what the sign said? I couldn't actually read the name. It was just that up until then all streets had names consisting of single words like Mary, Joyce, and Hope. I just looked for a sign that had two words instead of one.

Identifying a threat is usually easier than taking aim. It's not hard to locate someone coming at you with a knife, but if you are only trained to see a perfect sight picture before firing, you may someday run out of time before your attacker makes contact. If there's only about 25 percent of the amount of light you're used to having in order to perceive an adequate sight picture, the majority of the remaining 75 percent of your aiming information has to come from somewhere else. Just as I trusted my perception of a two word street name versus a single word when the letters weren't actually in focus, you've got to learn to pull together additional ways of confirming safe and effective aim.

I am sure some people would refer to this direction as developing the instinctual ability to aim, but I'd rather concentrate on learning more concrete ways to perceive positive aim. I am not sure he founded the teaching concept, but years ago the late Jim Cirillo asked students to practice shooting without the benefits of the sights on their pistols simply by covering the rear sight notch with black electrical tape before sending them to the firing line.[2] Cirillo was a member of the New York City Police Department's Stakeout

The rear sight of this Smith & Wesson 9mm M&P pistol has been covered with black electrical tape for the purpose of improving the shooter's ability to aim the gun properly. But whenever you practice, it is important to use only the most accurate and consistent ammunition available so the results are truly representative of your efforts. My experience as a firearms-test professional has taught me to rely upon Black Hills Ammunition.

Squad formed to counter a series of armed robberies and was the survivor of numerous shootouts at close range, often recounted as being reminiscent of the old west. In fact, his book *Guns, Bullets, and Gunfights* was subtitled *Tales From a Modern-Day Gunfighter*. Since then, many accomplished competitive shooters and tacticians have tried to quantify in writing just what happens when speed and accuracy are demanded under great stress.

Cirillo's method of taping over the sights is sure to help the shooter develop the ability to aim. I believe Cirillo's message was not merely that accuracy under fire was more than the sum of fundamental parts, I

believe it was that there are in fact more parts to be reckoned with than just the sights. With the sights covered, what else is there to tell if the gun is properly aligned?

The shooter learns not just what it looks like for the sights to be level, but what it feels like for the barrel of the gun to be parallel to the ground. If your rear sight has been taped over and you can still see the top of the front sight then you are aiming (and hitting) unnecessarily high.

If the gun is being held with the barrel pointing down, the front sight will not be visible and the hits will land lower than intended. Holding the gun

Practicing with the rear sight taped is not by any means like shooting with your eyes closed. It just means that instead of checking the sights, your vision is somewhat shared between the target and the rear face of the gun. To prove this, we began by mounting a LaserMax Micro II laser to our Springfield Armory XD9 Mod 2 and zeroed it to appear as a sunset just above the front sight.

With nothing more in view than the rear face of our Springfield Armory XD9 Mod 2, the gun is centered on target.

The splash of the LaserMax Micro II laser is perfectly centered but, with the top of the slide visible, the point of impact is well above the center of the target.

with the muzzle pointing slightly downward will also promote the practice of "scooping" the trigger, which will result in dipping the muzzle even further with each shot. This can be overcome by internalizing the sensation of locking the wrist at the proper angle.

Finger position on the trigger can affect accuracy by pulling or pushing one's aim off-center to the left or right. You can prove this to yourself without firing a shot by participating in laser training. Mount a laser on your unloaded pistol, then try to hold the laser point on the desired point of impact and pull the trigger. If the point doesn't move at all your trigger

press is true. Even if the dot moves during the press but is centered on your desired point of impact when the trigger breaks, you're achieving your goals.

With the sights taped there is still another visual point of reference available to the shooter. When the gun is aimed directly at the target, the back of the slide should appear with edges crisp, forming a more or less rectangular shape.

If the gun is aimed off-center to the left, a portion of the left side of the slide will be visible.

If the gun is being held or travels to the right side during trigger press, the right side of the slide will be visible and the resulting hits will likewise print to the right.

With the left side of the slide visible, the laser marks a virtual hit to the left of center.

With the right side of the slide visible, the laser marks a virtual hit to the right of center.

Once you've become accustomed to reading alignment without the sights, I recommend that you take Cirillo's methodology a little bit further. The typical range target is printed on white, tan, or an off-white color paper. The light thrown back at the shooter from the target is very helpful in judging alignment. To better help replicate low light conditions, leave the sights taped over but substitute the range target with its lines and circles for a piece of plain black construction paper. No rings and no bullseye. Paper the entire target board. Aim at a spot and fire several shots without stopping. A series of properly aligned shots should produce a group of holes closely knit together.

By denying visual access to the sights, the shooter is forced to look elsewhere for feedback indicating whether or not the shots are going where they want them to. We should all be familiar with the concept of calling our shots. Calling a shot is when you see the alignment of the sights on target at the moment the gun goes off and can accurately predict where the bullet hole will print. If the sights were off low and to the left, the hit will appear on target low and to the left. The bullet holes on target will always provide a map of the results of your alignment. When you can call a shot with a collection of feedback other than a perfect view of the sights, you are truly mastering your shooting skills.

Take A Test Drive

To gain access to a wide variety of guns, contact an instructor or visit a shooting range that rents guns. A salesperson in the typical gun store may also be able to show you a variety of guns but an instructor

Safety is accuracy. Only hits that strike the intended target are going to be effective in stopping the threat. Only hits that strike the intended target protect the innocent lives in the vicinity of the threat. Accuracy begins with familiarity and a natural fit to the hand. Familiarity can be learned, but how do you find out what gun is going to fit your hands best? Instead of buying one gun after another until you find the perfect gun, you can take a "Test Drive" with expert instructors like those found at Firearms Operations and Responsible Training of Texas (FortTexas.us). Training with F.O.R.T Texas on the scenic grounds of American Shooting Centers in Houston, Texas, you'll be able to shoot a wide variety of handguns to help you decide.

will be able to spend more time with you and answer more questions. Some professional training groups like Firearms Operations and Responsible Training of Texas (FortTexas.us) offer what they call a Test Drive class that gives each student the opportunity to shoot nearly every type of handgun and receive individual instruction specific to each design. Those who have never shot a gun before have the option of beginning with replica guns that project a beam of light rather than bullets. This helps reinforce safety habits and allows the student to focus on sight alignment and trigger control before having to deal with recoil. The Test Drive classes are popular with husbands and wives as well as small business owners that allow their employees to carry a concealed weapon. It's not only a great way to choose a gun but group classes ensure that each member of the staff or everyone in the family has the same training. Even if a husband and wife choose different guns they should at least have enough working knowledge to use each other's guns should one fail or run out of ammunition.

If you think a road test is strictly for beginners who have never shot or handled a gun before, you are mistaken. The types of guns people are familiar with is often generational. While writing a review for *Gun Tests* magazine comparing three lever action rifles, I decided to bring them to a casual shooting session with several friends who had just returned from military service. Their issued weapons were primarily the Beretta M9 semiautomatic pistol and the M4 carbine. The M4 carbine is similar in many ways to the civilian-available AR-15 platform but with the option of automatic fire. As it turned out only one of them had ever handled, let alone shot, a lever-action rifle. "My grandfather had one," he remembered. Furthermore, due to the popularity of the semiautomatic pistol, I wouldn't be surprised to meet adults younger than forty years of age who have never shot a revolver. Bear in mind that with the rarest of exceptions, every civilian weapon currently available started out as being designed for warfare. If anything, this should make you feel more confident no matter which system or style of gun you choose because they've all been road-tested in the heat of battle by America's best.

Hand Position for More Accurate Shooting

A high grip on the handgun offers more control over every aspect of shooting.

Choose a gun that allows you to hold the grip with the least amount of distance from the top of the hand to the bore axis (the center of the barrel).

A high grip allows the trigger finger to move with less deviation.

The greater the angle at which the trigger finger drops to the face of the trigger, the easier it will be to press the finger in a straight line.

Remember:

Only accurate shots on a verified threat will end aggression without putting others in danger.

Chapter 8 Safe Handling Practices in Awkward Situations

Once you understand and can perform the safe handling protocol specific to the design of your handgun as listed in the previous chapter, it is not difficult to avoid accidental discharge. In short, any handgun designed with an exposed hammer or a rotating cylinder will allow the operator to monitor unwanted movement of the trigger. Any handgun with a mechanical safety allows the operator to physically reinforce the safety in its on-safe position. The trigger of striker-fired pistols without a mechanical thumb safety should be monitored visually when holstering or whenever there's a possibility something could make contact with the trigger. In addition, pressing the thumb against the rear of the slide will help keep the slide of most pistols from moving out of battery to avoid a malfunction. If a grip-operated safety is present, then placing the thumb atop the rear of the slide will help make handling safer by leaving a gap below the web of the shooter's hand in order to avoid compressing the grip safety. It is important to utilize these methods habitually no matter what the distraction or how awkward the situation.

When it comes to handling a gun inside an automobile or getting it out of the way for a doctor's visit, massage therapy, or a trip to the men's room, awkward is the correct word, but not a new one. As listed in Webster's 1913 dictionary, entries found among the definitions for awkward include wanting (of) dexterity, causing inconvenience, embarrassing, and not at ease socially. The problem is that no matter the circumstance, awkwardness can be enough of a distraction to interfere with safe gun handling practices even if they are deep-seated enough to be considered habitual.

Notice that I referred to a trip to the men's room and said nothing about the ladies. That's because the vast majority of women carry their concealed weapons in a bag slung from the shoulder. As much as I'd like to see women find ways to carry on the belt so that a purse snatch is not also a gun grab, the habit of maintenance and control of one's handbag is an effective safeguard against leaving a sidearm behind in a restroom or anywhere else. I'm told that purse confiscation is going to be more difficult than gun confiscation because the incidence of women leaving behind a purse anywhere is almost unheard of if not unthinkable. One might ask if men should keep a shoulder bag or attaché case handy when they are going to the restroom while carrying a firearm. If this sounds like a good idea it might still be defeated by the absence of habit, leaving bag (and gun) behind. Sound impossible?

Men are not nearly as indoctrinated with carrying or maintaining control of shoulder bags as women are. I'm not able to come up a statistic of how many times a concealed-carry bag has been left in a supermarket shopping cart, but I've done it and been lucky enough to retrieve it upon my return. Ten steps outside of a restaurant, the SWAT operator I was having lunch with realized he had left his Vanquest EDC (Everyday Carry) Maximum Organizer hiding a Glock 26 in the booth where we'd been sitting. No matter how tactical the gear, men are just not wired like women are to be attached to a bag.

Women are far less likely than men to leave behind a gun carried in a purse than are men toting a pistol in the latest tactical shoulder bag. While most holsters are admittedly designed for the male body, the purse or shoulder bag is truly the women's domain. The Galco Pax is a perfect example of how well firearms can be integrated with women's couture. *Photo courtesy of Galco Gunleather.*

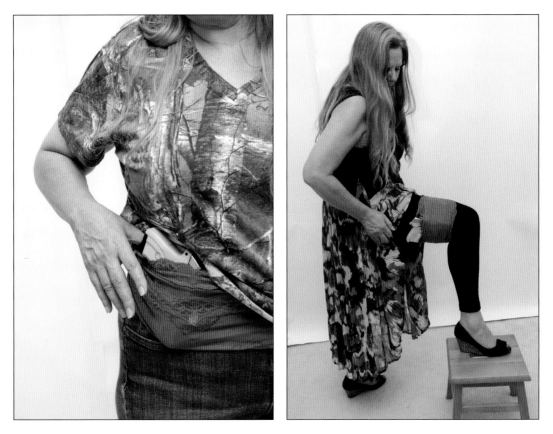

Few, if any, holsters are designed specifically for the female body. Add to this that women's clothing rarely utilizes a belt, let alone one sturdy enough for carrying a handgun. The Lethal Lace Universal Concealed Carry Holster provides a dedicated holster for small handguns that is integrated via decidedly feminine means. This enables the gun to be carried in numerous positions on the body including ankle, thigh, waist, and beneath the arm.

In July of 2014, the Rock Hill (South Carolina) *Herald* reported that a loaded Smith & Wesson .38 Special revolver was found on a toilet paper dispenser at a local Wal-Mart. The report says that a man had called police about the gun, described it accurately, and explained that he had indeed left it in the bathroom. Imagine having to make that call.[1]

In March of 2014, a Bridgeport, Connecticut, woman was charged with second-degree reckless endangerment after leaving a handgun in the ladies room of a Milford restaurant. The gun was discovered by an employee and turned over to police.[2] Thankfully, the restaurant staff was honest. The woman to whom the gun was registered was contacted by police and arrested. Whatever the penalties meted out in either of the above cases, I'd bet they got off cheap compared to anyone who might have been injured or killed should either of the guns been used in the commission of a crime. However, such negligence is not limited to private citizens. Even professionals have been accused of abandoning their firearms in the john.

The United States Capitol police were under the microscope during 2015 for losing control of duty guns, made worse by a photograph published on the *Roll Call* website. The photograph shows a Glock

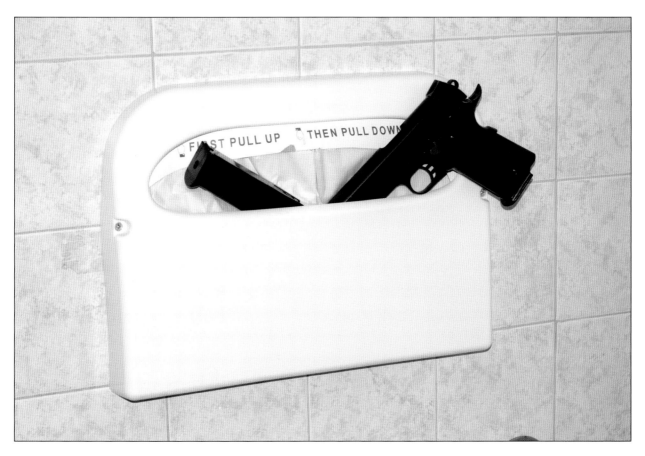

If you think the incidence of loaded guns left in restrooms is a fallacy, a photograph similar in content appeared in the news as recently as January of 2015 in connection to unattended Capitol Police handguns found in the restroom of a government building.

pistol and loaded magazine wedged into a toilet seat shield dispenser reportedly "inside the Senate office portion of the Capitol Visitor Center on Jan. 29, according to a source."[3] In the accompanying article, Hannah Hess wrote that "CQ Roll Call reported Friday three instances since January in which workers or, in one case, a child, have found unattended Capitol Police handguns—two left behind in bathrooms."[3] But at no point throughout the article is it established categorically that the weapon in the photograph belonged to police.

"I was unaware of these instances until this morning," said House Rules Chairman Pete Sessions, R-Texas. "The Capitol Hill Police are awesome people who need to retrain everyone that carries a gun. It does not surprise me that mistakes can be made, what would surprise me is if we did not retrain every single person with better procedures."

One might assume that the owner of the gun, if they were indeed a member of the Capitol Police, was dressed for undercover work or at least not wearing full uniform including a high retention holster. Here's why. While a shoulder holster system would offer less interference during a trip to the bathroom, the difficulty in controlling a weapon carried in the typical belt-mounted open top concealment holster could easily lead to the inappropriate practice of removing the pistol and magazine.

Referred to in the article as the "go-to guy" on police issues for the Administration Committee, former sheriff Rep. Rich Nugent, R-Florida, reportedly suggested looking at better technology, such as lockboxes, to be taken into the bathroom. Would that mean a wall of lockers or a lock box in each stall? Personally, I have never been in a bathroom outside of my own home in which I felt so comfortable that I could bring myself to take off even a Cub Scout ring and leave it by the sink. But if I were tasked with training plainclothes police or

citizens how to maintain control of their concealed carry sidearms, there are some practices I would ask them to consider.

First of all, at no time should the weapon leave the holster. The gun and the holster should be handled as a unit. If the operator is wearing a shoulder holster or harness system, the unit should stay on the body. Pull the shirttails up and fold them over the holster to keep the unit close to the body.

If the operator is wearing a belt-mounted holster, the gun, holster, and strong side of the waistband

For anyone wearing a shoulder holster rig, removing the gun in a restroom is seldom necessary. Concealment and control can be maintained by merely folding the shirttails up and over the unit.

It's easy to appear at ease and maintain concealment when wearing a shoulder holster because the outline of the gun does not follow the hips nor weigh down the belt.

must be held together as a single unit as you lower your pants. I offer the following step-by-step example that you may be able to improve upon, but the key is to control the gun at all times without removing it from the holster. You must also recognize the necessity of reconnecting the belt.

The process of lowering the pants begins with unzipping the fly, then disconnecting the button above the zipper. The belt stays connected. The next step is to grasp the gun and holster as a unit. Thumb on the inside of the pant pressing against the inner side of the holster. The fingers are on the outside of the holster with the web of the hand bridging over the back of the slide. Do not grasp the handle of the gun. The gun and holster are always handled as a unit even if the holster is clipped to the inside batting of the pants alone.

Disconnect the belt without letting go of the holster/gun unit using your weak side (non-gun side) hand.

One way to reduce the risk of your gun falling out of the holster when lowering your pants is to grip the holster, gun, pants, and belt as one. Buckling the belt provides additional control.

Return the weak side hand to the opposite side of the pants and sit down. Maintain a grip on the gun/holster unit and reconnect the belt, applying pressure by spreading your legs to keep the gun upright.

When the time comes to stand up, take hold of the gun/holster unit, unlatch the belt, return the weak hand to the opposite side of the pants and pull up as you stand. You may have to immediately refasten your belt, but the key is to control both sides of the pants as you zip up and reconnect the top button.

If you can find a shortcut around some of the above step-by-step instructions, the one practice that shouldn't be skipped is how the gun and holster are handled as one piece. Be aware that even a snap retention or locking holster will not prevent the unit from flopping over and hitting the floor, hence the need for refastening the belt.

If there were any acceptable variation from the instruction to not separate the gun from the holster, it would be the following, but be sure to pay attention to the second part of the process. It is inevitable when traveling to stop to use a public restroom. And it is certain that you will from time to time be invited out to a restaurant. Consider keeping a shoulder bag in the car for temporary transfer. Certainly more and more people are keeping a "bug-out" bag filled with emergency items inside their cars, but what I like to call a temporary transfer bag does not necessarily need to be elaborate. In fact, a low-profile bag of common appearance is probably a better idea than one offering a military or tactical style. Make sure it has a zippered compartment somewhere in the interior. Nothing else should share this compartment. Better yet, you can buy a separate panel that fits inside the bag that includes a holster. There may be slots for spare magazines as well. Some panels are backed with heavy Velcro so the matching holster can be positioned and canted to match the bag. Bring the bag with you to the restroom. In choosing a private

stall, check to see that it has a hook on the back of the door. Place the gun inside the bag and hang it directly in front of you.

If you think having the gun directly in front of you and/or located between yourself and the exit is not essential, there is one small detail about the Glock pistol and magazine left behind in the January 2015 incident at the Capitol Visitor Center. While not explicitly stated in the caption, the seat guard dispenser is shown mounted on a tiled wall. This is an important detail because solid walls are more often than not in position behind the toilet and "out of sight out of mind" could very easily have played a part in this incident. Whether or not this assumption is true, multiple cases of guns left behind in restrooms proves that it is possible to become mentally numb to the responsibility of maintaining control of one's firearms.

Keeping a temporary transfer bag can come in handy for situations other than when meeting personal needs. For example, a trip to massage therapy will require disrobing. So would a trip to the doctor's office for even a routine examination. Leaving the gun holstered and hidden beneath a pile of clothing is ill-advised and irresponsible in my opinion. Some may choose to hide their personal defense gun inside the car before entering the facility, but this is also not a good idea. Leaving a gun unattended in a car is always risky, but first let's focus on the risk of not having it with you for your appointment. Structurally, a licensed commercial massage therapy business consists of little more than a series of small rooms connected by one or more hallways. The interior is kept in varying degrees of reduced lighting for the purpose of relaxing the patient. (A small flashlight, handheld or capable of being attached to the handgun, should also be kept in your temporary transfer bag.) At any moment, most of the people inside are at least partially undressed and lying down, increasing vulnerability. No way am I leaving my gun in the car.

Leaving a personal defense gun behind when using the restroom is a much more pervasive problem than anyone is willing to admit. Problems begin when the weapon is removed from the holster without anywhere to store it. If you should choose to store it temporarily in a briefcase, purse, or shoulder bag, just make sure you hang it up on the back of the bathroom stall door or in full view of the exit so it doesn't get left behind.

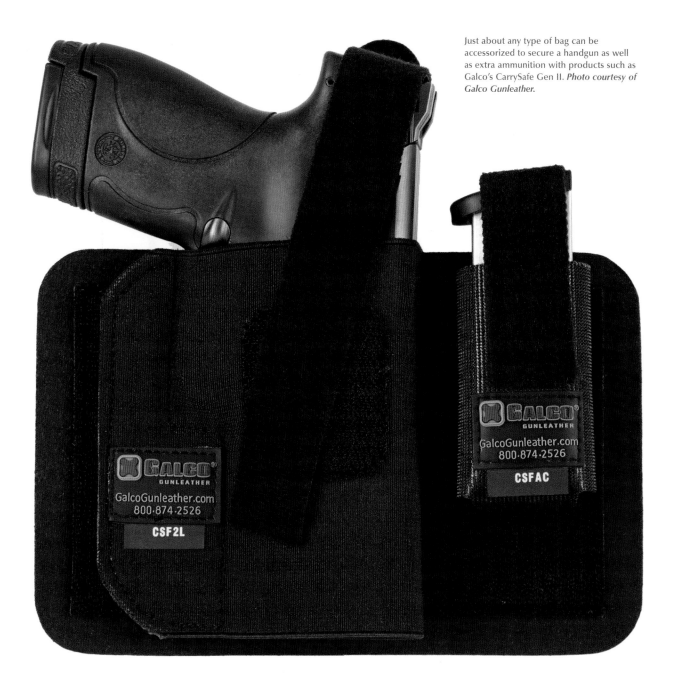

Leaving firearms in an automobile is a crapshoot. Not letting anyone know there are firearms in the vehicle in the first place is important but it's not always possible to keep a secret. Automobiles themselves can be secured, but access to the interior is not difficult. Furthermore, any gun left in a position that can be quickly accessed is not going to be difficult to find. Small safes can be bolted into the glove box and secure compartments such as those made by TruckVault can be installed.

Professionals that keep an emergency arsenal have a designated area but these reinforced drawers and boxes do not make the weapons immediately available without exiting the vehicle. Nevertheless, there are circumstances when one's concealed-carry firearm must be left inside the car.

Automobiles themselves can be secured, but access to the interior is not difficult. This means guns lefts behind are at risk of being stolen. The best way to ensure security when you must leave your gun inside a vehicle is to install a high-quality safe. TruckVault, a leader in the field, offers the ShotLock Console quick-access safe specifically for this purpose. *Photo courtesy of TruckVault.*

It should be expected that certain facilities are off-limits for personal firearms even when in possession of a state-issued concealed handgun permit. Such facilities include hospitals (but not necessarily a professional building attached to the hospital), most sports arenas and stadiums, plus any event where there is wagering. It's easy to see the reason why since they can all be emotionally-charged environments. In the case of hospitals, that's not the entire reason. While gunshot victims and perpetrators alike (rival gang members, for example) have been known to mete out revenge right there in the emergency room, the original reason for banning guns in hospitals stems from it being an oxygen-rich environment. With so many patients directly or indirectly being fed high quantities of O2, there is risk of explosion. Public schools (at least the building interiors or in some states simply the grounds outside the boundaries of your automobile) are generally off-limits as well. Other establishments include privately owned businesses, bars, and restaurants that either derive at least 51% of their income from the sale of alcohol or otherwise choose to deny entry so long as they post a sign with the proper quotation of law clearly in view of the entrance. It is the responsibility of each citizen to know how the laws apply in their city or wherever they travel. Every citizen, armed or otherwise, has the choice to spend their time and money in establishments that believe its patrons have the right to defend themselves, which is what the Second Amendment essentially boils down to.

Other than the necessity of visiting the hospital, I don't recommend anyone willingly patronize a gun-free zone. But there are times when the necessity to visit a facility that is off-limits to carrying a firearm comes up unexpectedly or the visit comes at an interval that fills just a few minutes out of a highly-active day. The gun or guns must be handled safely without attracting attention, and stowed out of sight if not secured under lock and key. Using the techniques outlined in the previous chapter should be helpful but let's examine some of the specific challenges to handling a firearm inside of a car. Not during a gunfight, mind you, but administratively as in the course of normal operations.

Removing the gun from your mode of carry should not begin until the car is stopped and the car is placed in park. You should already have performed a visual search of the general area before choosing a parking space. (Actually, your surveillance or rather countersurveillance of who is watching you should remain ongoing.) Parking areas are for people coming and going. Populace in motion should be the norm. Someone standing around looking at the cars would be one red flag. Anyone walking around aimlessly without keys in their hands would be another. The body language of other people in a parking lot should reflect some level of concern. Be wary of anyone who is not putting away their keys and taking stock of their belongings. People seen approaching parked cars with packages from the adjoining store would be an appropriate sight. Anyone motionless should stand out.

Taking a moment to look forward, left, right, and to the rear before turning off the engine is always a good idea, but don't forget to look at the interior of cars right next to you. If you intend to put up a sunscreen behind the windshield to provide extra security for your actions, do it before making a move for your handgun.

You should be familiar with boundaries in your car such as the center console, steering wheel, column mounted selector, or stick shift. Typically, the seat belt is the first source of constriction. With the luxury of already being parked, you can release the seat belt before taking the gun out of the holster. Even if your gun is in a briefcase or bag next to you, unbuckling the seat belt will give you more freedom to move. The question of where to stow the handgun should already be determined. The best option for retention is a lockable safe bolted beneath the seat or to the interior of the glove box.

No matter where you place the gun, position it so that access from the driving position promotes a normal strong-hand grip with the muzzle pointing away from you. The same way you place the gun down is the same way you will pick it up, with index finger straight alongside the frame or cylinder and the thumb at the rear of the slide or atop the hammer. Make sure there is nothing loose inside the compartment that can find its way inside the trigger guard or barrel. This would include loose change, any sort of small object such as nuts and bolts, keys, pencils, or trash such as a wadded-up candy wrapper. Think of this space as your holster and recognize that, for the time being at least, it has no other purpose than to maintain a clear opportunity for presentation of the weapon. It's okay to place something over the gun so that it is not immediately visible when opening the compartment. A cardboard CD cover or small notebook works well as long as there are no loose ends dangling that could get inside the trigger guard or snag on to the weapon. Otherwise, make sure there is nothing around the gun that can block your hand from retrieving it.

Safely returning the gun from its hiding place inside the car to one's mode of carry is more challenging if for no other reason than change of direction. As the gun is being pulled from a holster or compartment, the predominant movement is to the rear and anything that contacts the trigger is more likely to push it forward which is in the opposite direction to a press towards ignition. Shoving the gun into a holster causes anything that contacts the trigger to push dangerously to the rear. Before placing the gun into the holster, look at the opening to make sure it is clear. If you are going to put the gun inside a briefcase or purse compartment, clear the opening first but do so before picking up the gun.

Don't cheat by holding the gun in one hand while probing the compartment with the other. Beyond the likelihood of sympathetic hand movement (in a moment of stress or even mild surprise it is common for the actions of one hand to duplicate the actions of the other), you're probably going

to need a second hand to inspect and/or clear the interior anyway.

In handling the gun as it is returned to the holster, remember that striker-fired guns with nothing more than a trigger-mounted safety will need to be looked into the holster. Many "high speed, low drag" operators preach that you can bypass this step by learning the correct angle to insert the handgun, but I've caught just as many giving the mouth of the holster a quick look. If anyone tells you that concentrating on forward vision while reholstering ensures against an emerging threat, tell them you prefer to keep the gun out in a ready position until it is more positively clear. Simply put, a great many accidental discharges occur upon holstering and there is more to fear from being careless than there is to not appearing to be cool.

With so much emphasis on safe administrative handling inside your vehicle, I would be remiss if I didn't offer some key advice on making it easier to draw the gun. If you've ever timed your draw from a seated position it was probably without a seat belt in place or the effects of wearing a cover garment. Even if you live in a state where open carry can be practiced legally, at some point you're going to

Handling firearms quickly within the confines of an automobile presents a number of problems, not the least of which is the steering wheel. Be prepared to move the gun in an arc over the top of the steering wheel to avoid catching the muzzle as you move toward point of aim.

Reholstering while seated inside a car is not the time to try to look cool and show off that no-look holstering technique you've been practicing. Perhaps if the operator had taken the time to look he would have seen that the knife in his pocket was pressing up against the slide of his pistol and pushing the barrel out of battery. But if the operator had placed his thumb atop the rear of the slide before holstering, he certainly would have felt the resistance and repaired the situation. Whenever possible, such as when parked, put up a sun shield for added privacy and take your time to handle the gun safely.

be wearing a sweater or sweatshirt, leaving your shirt-tails untucked, or wearing a jacket to suit the weather. Once you take your position in the vehicle with seat belt in place, you'll probably need to pull a portion of your garment from beneath the belt or from wherever it may be bound. If you do not preset a clear path of access to your gun, you're going to add seconds to your draw, not to mention an edge of confusion or even desperation to the process. In addition, the act of pulling clear any such garments can serve as a furtive action, giving notice to whoever is watching that you are drawing a weapon. Naturally, you shouldn't actually draw unless you are threatened, but if you can put your hand on the gun cleanly without drawing attention you will be all the more ready.

Safe Handling in Awkward Places
Checklist

Never separate a gun from its holster outside of your home or automobile.

Exception:
Should it become necessary to remove a gun from a holster in a bathroom (public or private) place the gun immediately in a shoulder bag, purse, or briefcase.
Hang the bag on the inside of the stall door or on the door handle on the interior side of the bathroom exit.
Do not place a bag or briefcase containing a gun in a shopping cart.

If you must leave a handgun inside your vehicle temporarily:

Create a designated position inside your car for temporary concealed storage of your handgun.

Adapt a lockable compartment within reach of the driver's seat.

Make sure any storage compartment is free of loose items that can travel inside the trigger guard.

Make sure any storage compartment is clean and free of small items that can enter into the action of the firearm.

Position the firearm so that it is accessible via a secure finger off trigger pre-shooting grip.

When reholstering or rebagging while seated inside a vehicle:

Check to see if the holster or bag is clear before picking up the handgun.

Attain a safe grip with index finger outside the trigger guard.

Look the gun all the way into the holster whether it is belt-mounted or inside a dedicated carry compartment.

When seated in a vehicle with a holstered gun, make sure your clothing does not bind or otherwise hinder a direct path to the gun.

Chapter 9 Commuting and the Road Rage Phenomena

"The enormity of the task of driving is the power of life or death."

—R. Eckstine

When the famous words "Houston, we have a problem" were uttered by Apollo mission astronauts, NASA technicians went to work solving problems using a computer with the capacity of only 32k of memory (32,000 bits). Never mind today's smartphone or the Apple watch, technology of the era paled in comparison even to toy-like achievements such as the Casio digital watch. We've come a long way in terms of technology, but when it comes to human interaction there are still certain situations that cause us to trip and fall suddenly from the precipice of our modern civilized world into a jungle of chaos. Suddenly finding yourself in the midst of road rage is just such an event.

What is it that makes road rage so alarming? Oftentimes one participant (the aggressor) is fully motivated while the victim is completely surprised. The really odd thing is that road rage is a relatively modern phenomenon. According to a National Highway Traffic Safety Administration report (NHTSA DOT HS 809 707) published in 2004, "Until the final decade of the Twentieth Century, most motorists were comforted by knowing that aggressive driving behavior was infrequent and atypical, and that extreme, confrontational acts were quite rare."[1] What has changed?

According to the office of the Washington State Patrol (the State of Washington's Highway Patrol),

"Society is moving at a faster pace now more than ever. It is possible the increased value of time is causing us to be much more aggressive on the road, especially during commuting hours. Some drivers only see the traffic ahead of them as an obstacle to overcome at any cost. When we couple this with society becoming accustomed to instantaneous communications, the problem becomes more pronounced. Whatever the reasons may be this attitude can place those who share the roadway in jeopardy."[2]

Before continuing, we should be aware of two basic definitions as per the NHTSA:

Aggressive Driving
"The commission of two or more moving violations that is likely to endanger other persons or property, or any single intentional violation that requires a defensive reaction of another driver."[3]

Road Rage
"An assault with a motor vehicle or other dangerous weapon by the operator or passenger(s) of one motor vehicle on the operator or passenger(s) of another motor vehicle caused by an incident that occurred on a roadway."[4]

Aggressive driving can lead to road rage but the possibility of the line between the two being blurred is very real. The important distinction between the two is that aggressive driving is a traffic violation and road rage is a criminal offense. Does anyone set out to commit road rage or is it the result of behaviors that are tested and inflamed? Inside the NHTSA report cited above, we learn that "The words, 'aggressive driving' emerged during the 1990s as a label for a category of dangerous on-the-road behaviors" and that "aggressive driving occasionally escalates to gesturing in anger or yelling at another motorist, confrontation, physical assault and even murder; 'Road Rage' is the label that emerged to describe the angry and violent behaviors at the extreme of the aggressive driving continuum."[5]

The aggressive driving continuum is a fancy, if not "sci-fi" sounding term, that in my interpretation suggests that as aggression mounts between two or more drivers, the possibility of crossing the threshold from aggressive driving to that of road rage can increase in a crescendo-like fashion. Better yet, think of the aggressive driving continuum as a speedometer with a driver's emotions in check on the low end and violent behavior at the other. This illustration is validated by a definition of the word continuum found in Webster's online dictionary ending with a tag attributed to historian Wayne Shumaker: "good" and "bad" . . . stand at opposite ends of a *continuum* instead of describing the two halves of a line."[6] Keeping this in mind, the key to surviving a road rage incident is not to allow your emotions to "peg" the needle on the speedometer and lose control.

How you react to an aggressive driving or road rage confrontation can create a competition between yourself and the other driver. Certainly any action such as flipping off the other driver is going to send the needle on the continuum meter zooming. This is easily understood. But what are some of the conditions of everyday life that set us up for overreacting due to anger or anxiety just below the surface of our composure?

When it comes to "the increased value of time causing us to be much more aggressive on the road," being delayed has become a big issue and so has invasion of privacy. Phone and internet connection may very well be reducing both our attention span and setting us up for failure in situations that call for patience. Add to this the fact that today's automobiles do everything they can to accommodate the driver and insulate them from the environment, perhaps causing us to become territorial while driving, as if we're riding around in our own little castles. The prevalence of air conditioning means that we drive with windows rolled up, reducing the sensation of speed and removing much of the ability of the driver to hear the vehicles around us, especially when they are approaching from the rear. It's no wonder that many road rage or aggressive driving incidents begin with vastly different interpretations of what's needed to safely negotiate traffic. One driver might think flashing their lights or sounding the horn is doing the other driver a favor, but another driver takes such warnings as an insult or a challenge. In the end, there are certain behaviors that leave you open to attracting the attention of drivers that are on the edge emotionally and looking to take out whatever problem they have in their personal lives on whoever seems vulnerable at the time.

One study of the causation of aggressive driving that was not commissioned by the government but instead by a private entity comes to us from Expedia, a company well-known on the Internet that offers discounts related to the travel industry. John Morrey, Vice President and General Manager of Expedia.com says, "Expedia rents millions of cars to Americans, so we set out to learn what behaviors on the open road are most welcome, and what behaviors most aggravating. The rule, as with airplanes and hotels, is that shared spaces demand decorum and attentiveness."[7] According to this report ranked as the most "annoying or offensive" driving behaviors are the following:

The Texter (drivers who text, e-mail, or talk on a phone while driving): 69%,
The Tailgater (drivers who follow others far too closely): 60%,

The Multi-tasker (applying makeup, eating, reading, etc.): 54%,

The Drifter (either straddling two lanes or weaving between them): 43%,

The Crawler (driving well below the speed limit): 39%,

The Swerver (failing to signal before changing lanes or turning): 38%,

The Left-Lane Hog (drivers who occupy the passing lane without moving): 32%,

The Inconsiderate (those who do not let others merge): 30%,

The Speeder (driving well past the speed limit at length): 27%,

The Honker (drivers who slam the horn at will): 18%,

The Unappreciative (drivers who do not give a wave or gesture of thanks): 13%, and

The Red Light Racer (drivers who inch ever closer to the light when red): 12%.[8]

If you have ever engaged in any of the above behaviors, you are sure to have drawn the ire of other drivers at one time or another. The Expedia study points out that distraction is the most infuriating behavior but it is easy to cure. The first step to avoid being distracted is to take on the attitude that when you are driving it is your job to drive and you owe it to your "customers" to follow a code of conduct. When I was a professional driver for hire, I didn't try to buddy up with my fares on passenger trips. I set the tone at introduction saying, "My name is Roger and I will be providing safe transport for you and your guests." This meant I would take on the responsibility of protecting them from the dangers inherent to driving among less-qualified and unpredictable operators.

Unfortunately, the time people spend in the day driving between destinations is often looked upon as downtime or being wasteful. But it wasn't always so. Years ago, salesmen enjoyed the ride between calls.

Being inside an automobile meant they were unavailable. Then the pager came on the scene. Today they wouldn't think of just sitting behind the wheel without checking e-mail or making a phone call. Somehow, the availability of social media seems to have made being out of contact undesirable. Technology not only tempts us to divide our attention but trains us that multitasking is appropriate for every waking moment. Maybe it's gotten to the point where everyone who has a driver's license should be issued a chauffeur's cap and ordered to wear it every time they drive so they can be reminded to make driving their first priority as if it was a job. Approaching even the shortest trip as a professional driver will make you more vigilant and a safer all-around driver.

Choosing Routes to Avoid Confrontation

As a commuter you most likely take the same route to and from work with little variation. The same goes for running regular errands to the supermarket or gasoline station, etc. Have you chosen the safest route? If you travel roads with higher speed limits, does your route require you to cross oncoming traffic in order to turn into a parking lot or change directions? Does the route require you to make a U-turn or perform a sudden merge in a short amount of time or distance? Are you ever forced to make a decision when to cross oncoming traffic or is there another place to turn that is controlled by a traffic light? Is there any intersection or point of yield that repeatedly contributes to an inordinate amount of traffic accidents? After just a few trips to and from on your daily commute to work or shopping, you should be well-aware of trouble spots along the route that might cause you to have a close call or disagreement with another driver.

Reducing Stress to Short-circuit Aggression

Most of the advice coming from official sources focuses on how to avoid being engaged in an aggressive driving or road rage incident has to do with creating a stress-free environment resulting in a non-competitive atmosphere. Widely recognized safety tips include the following:

1. Allow plenty of time for the trip, listen to soothing music, improve the comfort in your vehicle, and understand that you cannot control the traffic, only your reaction to it.
2. In the end, we may very well discover that personal frustration, anger, and impatience may be the most dangerous "drugs" on the highway.
3. Be polite and courteous, even if the other driver is not. Avoid all conflict if possible.
4. When entering traffic or changing lanes, make sure you have enough room.
5. Make sure you have established a safe following distance between your vehicle and the one in front of you.
6. Signal when turning or changing lanes.
7. Put yourself in the other driver's shoes. They may be driving that way because of an actual emergency!

As with most advice and written law, the above was designed primarily for law-abiding citizens in a normal mindset free of agitation. The problem is that aggressive driving that can lead to road rage is the result of a highly-charged emotional state of mind. Allowing plenty of time is good advice but don't allow yourself to be spoiled. Soothing music and comfort are great for quieting the mind, but try turning off the judgmental portion of your mind. As a day shift yellow cab driver in New York City, I expected the worst-possible traffic to be beyond my imagination. In the midst of questionable actions by other drivers, concentrate on remaining vigilant; operate the car as necessary but with a sense of always waiting and watching.

I like the reference to personal frustration, anger, and impatience being maybe the most dangerous "drugs"

on the highway. You wouldn't think of downing a fifth of vodka and driving home would you? Then don't drive when agitated. Nor would you go to work just so you could punch your boss in the face, would you? Think of driving as a job you don't want to lose.

The list continues:

8. If another driver challenges you, take a deep breath and move out of the way.
9. Never underestimate the other driver's capacity for mayhem.
10. Don't make aggressive hand gestures to other drivers.
11. Control your anger; remember it takes two to start a fight.
12. Avoid prolonged eye contact with a bad or angry driver.
13. Get help. Call police on your cell phone or go to a public telephone or place. Don't pull to the side of the road.
14. Forget about winning. No one wins in a highway crash.

With the exception of tip number 13, tips 8 through 14 deal with mindset. It all goes back to being vigilant to the brink of detachment. Doing what needs to be done without emotion. But how do you not get upset when someone is being aggressive? You remain vigilant and implement sensible, planned actions. The parallel between surviving a criminal attack such as road rage to fighting in the ring or in the Octagon is worthwhile if you are willing to learn from professional fighters. On the professional level, emotion has very little to do with winning a fight. Sure, we see fighters calling each other out with insults and challenges before the fists fly but that's just to entice more people watch the fight. Once inside the ropes the process is much more cerebral.

Probably the most famous quote regarding a fighter's ability to think and apply skills without the distraction of emotion comes from martial arts icon Bruce Lee in the 1973 film *Enter the Dragon*. Nose to nose with a menacing competitor, Lee is asked, "What's your style?" He calmly answers, "My style? You can call it the art of fighting without fighting." In real-life professional mixed martial arts (MMA), fighter Daniel Weichel of Germany came within seconds of earning a title but was knocked out just when it looked like he would complete a masterful win. A veteran of more than professional fights, Weichel revealed the depth of his own wisdom by telling reporters in a subsequent interview that the reason he had lost was, "I got too emotional. I lost my cool. And I paid the price." In much the same way a fighter can be distracted by emotion, anyone thinking of getting back at another driver for being cut off will likely miss their chance to escape and be in danger of the event spiraling out of control.

Choose the Proper Lane

Not every incident of aggressive driving is caused by poor mindset or bad behavior. Sometimes managing your driving to fit the road can itself prevent close calls.

What we're looking to avoid is unnecessary interaction, especially those that can frustrate, surprise, or unintentionally threaten another driver. This starts with reducing the possibility of a collision or close call. Anytime you are on a road with two or more lanes in your direction of travel, use the following to dictate your choice of lane. Let's start with how you prioritize the lanes on a highway with three lanes in each direction. The lane closest to the shoulder should be for entry and exit from the flow of traffic. The center lane is for maintaining a steady speed and is where you should spend most of your travel time. The inside lane or the lane closest to oncoming traffic is for passing. Here's why.

The outer lane (the lane closest the shoulder) is also the lane that is directly up against the flow of traffic from streets that run into the highway. There are also driveways and exits from parking lots that are necessarily positioned on the right-hand edge of the outer lane. Anyone entering the highway is going to be turning into this lane. This means they will initially be going much slower than you and when they are in the process of turning they will be looking away from you as they do so. If you are cruising in the outer lane you will be subject to multiple slowdowns as cars turn on to the highway. This will raise your frustration level. Traveling in the outer lane repeatedly puts you directly in the path of other drivers making decisions based on your speed and on their own building sense of urgency that they have to get going on the way to their destination. By cruising in the outer lane, you are in danger because cars will be constantly cutting in front of you. This is frustrating for you and for anyone trying to merge with traffic. When you travel in the outside lane you are increasing the probability of interaction with other drivers under stress.

The inside lane (the lane closest to the opposite flow of traffic) is best used for passing. I could add that you could use this lane for excessive speed but that would be irresponsible. Nevertheless, we all know that people exceed the speed limit all the time, so even if you are traveling at the speed limit expect to be passed by other cars. For maintaining a steady speed, choose the center lane.

When traveling on a highway with two lanes in each direction, it is still wise to choose the inside lane for passing and maintaining a steady speed. Drive the speed limit and check your rearview mirrors for anyone coming up behind you. If your rearview and sideview mirrors are properly set, they should be easily visible via peripheral vision. If you see someone speeding up behind you, immediately put on your right side turn signal to indicate you are willing to get out of the way. Here is the crucial moment. Be prepared to wait after activating the turn signal and look for signs that the driver coming up behind you has acknowledged your offer to move over. This would be indicated by a noticeable reduction in speed on their part. What you must avoid is moving over quickly. Even if you activate your blinker without acknowledgement from the other driver, this can be taken as cutting him off. Unless the signal for change of lane has been acknowledged, you will likely suffer an emotional overreaction based on the frustration of "Hey, I signaled I was getting out of the way." Then you would be competing, pitting your frustration against the other driver.

Blowing the Horn

Blowing the horn is another source of irritation that can lead to an aggressive response from other drivers. It's difficult to argue that it's necessary to blow the horn reflexively to avoid collision, but there are times when it is used more as an expression of frustration than as a signal in an emergency. A good example of how using the horn can get you in trouble is when the light turns green and the delay before moving is perceived as being too long. Let's look at this from more than one side.

Ideally, everyone waiting at the light should take on an attitude governed first and foremost by safety. When the light turns green, it doesn't necessarily mean traffic in the other directions has come to a halt. There is always someone who will try to get through even when the yellow or amber light, which is supposed to warn drivers that the green light period is about to end, has been showing for some time and the red light will likely appear before they can cross the intersection. This is often the result of inattention by drivers but in many cases simply a matter of ego. A famous story told by Indianapolis 500 legend Bobby Unser describes being interviewed by a reporter as they rode through his hometown of Albuquerque, New Mexico. Bobby was bragging about how he and his brother Al, also a legendary racer, considered themselves so famous and untouchable in the city of Albuquerque they never bothered to stop for a red light because there wasn't a cop in town that would give them a ticket. To his surprise, the writer suddenly jammed on the brakes before the very next light. The writer explained, "What if Al is coming from the other direction?" Expect people to run red lights even right in front of you. That's what drivers do. Wait for it, look for it, and maybe even keep count of how often it happens just for amusement. Do anything but get angry about it.

When it comes to stoplights, the key to not developing an adversarial relationship that can lead to road rage is to build in a degree of patience. I have sometimes been guilty of treating the stoplight as if it were the "Christmas tree" or "go" lights at a drag strip. Here's how I overcame my quick trigger impulse to blow the horn. Hold the steering wheel with your hands some distance from the pressure point that sounds the horn. When the light changes, tap your fingers on the steering wheel to expend the nervous energy. This will give you enough time to decide (rather than act via reflex) whether or not it's really necessary to blow the horn. The driver at the head of the line (who by the way has the best view of crossing traffic) should be prepared to react to the green light in much the same way. Give it a time-out. Taking an extra second to check for a clear intersection can save lives. And again, any time you can avoid a near miss you're preventing the opportunity for emotions to trigger an incident of road rage.

Blowing the horn reflexively in reaction to a dangerous situation can be just as provocative as leaning on the horn and menacing every driver that gets in your way. But we've all done it and justifiably so. How many times has the other driver thanked you? See if you can identify with the driver in the following interview conducted in November of 2015. The name is fictitious but the incident is not.

RE: What time of day was it when the incident began?

Laura: Oh, it was daylight. About 3:30 p.m. last August. I remember how hot it was so naturally I had the windows up and the air conditioner running.

RE: What kind of car were you driving?

Laura: A Lincoln sedan. It's a big car, the kind they used to make.

RE: Who was with you?

Laura: I was by myself.

RE: How did it happen?

Laura: It was where Highway 36 merges with 59.

RE: Go on.

Laura: It's where two lanes go to one in each direction. There's also a center lane for turning left. What I mean is the right-hand lane continues straight but the inside lane turns into a left turn only lane so anyone in the left-hand lane has to merge from the center lane over a very short distance. It comes up really suddenly.

RE: So you had to swerve into the right-hand lane?

Laura: No. I was in the right-hand lane all along. All of sudden a car came up fast on my left and cut me off to get in front of me. I gave him a quick horn.

RE: What did the driver look like?

Laura: A young male driving a small blue sedan.

RE: What did he do next?

Laura: He slowed down to about 20 mph. We (meaning all the cars behind me) had been going about 50 mph so he was holding up a line of cars, not just me.

RE: Did he slow to a stop or try to stop short in front of you?

Laura: No. He pulled into the turn lane and signaled to make a left turn.

RE: So you thought it was over.

Laura: Before I could think anything, he came back to the right to cut me off.

He got right beside me and pushed me over.

RE: Did he hit your car?

Laura: No. I got out of his way but had to leave the shoulder to do it. Then he let me in front of him so I accelerated to get away but he kept pace. He tried to hit me and then he left.

RE: Were you armed?

Laura: Yes. My gun was in my purse beside me on the seat.

RE: What kind of gun did you have with you?

Laura: A Smith & Wesson 642. [Note: It is a small five-shot revolver with lightweight alloy frame chambered for .38 Special ammunition.]

RE: Would you have been able to get the gun out?

Laura: I had the gun in the zipper pocket that runs along the side. It's not actually a concealed-carry type purse but I did have the gun pointed forward in the proper direction.

RE: Meaning?

Laura: Facing forward. So I could access it directly with a shooting grip.

RE: Did you access the gun?

Laura: No, but I didn't want him beside me. I thought to myself [that] if he gets beside me like window to window or continued to pursue me I was going to take it out.

RE: Did you call 911 during or after the incident?

Laura: I was too busy. And after he left, I watched for him to return all the way home. I was hyped up for long time after.

RE: How long do you think the incident lasted?

Laura: Well, I'm pretty sure we averaged a mile a minute (60 mph). Seemed like three or four minutes. But the next time I went down that way, the distance from where it first started to where I exited wasn't that far at all. So I really don't know. One thing's for sure.

RE: What's that?

Laura: I relive it every time I go through that intersection.

The incident was triggered when Laura sounded the car horn in response to the perpetrator aggressively cutting in front of her. Sounding the horn was an understandable, if not instinctive, reaction. But instead of taking it as a warning of a possible collision, the other driver perceived it as an act of aggression. Certainly, anyone looking for a fight or at least some way to prove a point is ripe for being aggravated to the point of aggression, but this could also be explained as predatory behavior. This goes with the tough self image or "machismo" often cited in reports profiling the character of aggressive drivers. Such drivers are difficult to spot because until the predator on the highway strikes, their car looks like any other. In effect, they are camouflaged until the action of driving aggressively distinguishes their presence.

Whereas Laura felt that sounding the car horn was an act of assertion, the predatory personality may very well have interpreted it as a sign of fear, feeding his aggression. Studies show that women and older, weaker-looking people are more often the targets of road rage. Add to this the fact that Laura was driving a big car that, despite being an older model, could still be seen as a sign of wealth. If this sounds far-fetched, note that studies such as the Mizell report prepared for the AAA Foundation for Traffic Safety that studied some ten thousand reported cases of road rage offers the following: "The car is symbolic in many ways, regardless of its owner's perception of it."[9] In addition, it is not uncommon to find sentiments of class warfare, lower income versus the affluent, to also play a part according to several studies.

As the incident progressed, there were several opportunities for it to spiral out of control. First of all, let's consider whether this was a case of aggressive driving, which is a traffic violation, or did it rise to the level of criminal offense? Under the law, it would be at the very least reckless driving unless it could be proven that the other driver had used the car as a weapon. Indeed he had, but since Laura's car was not damaged, proof of what would amount, to a charge of aggravated assault (assault with a deadly weapon) would depend on an eyewitness account, or if Laura had video evidence such as from a dashboard-mounted camera. If she had not been alone, her passenger might have been able to photograph or even videotape the incident using a smart phone.

Road rage is among the most underreported of all crimes and probably the least likely to be thwarted by police intervention. Because both victim and perpetrator are traveling in moving vehicles, not only is the location of the crime constantly in flux but the complainant has their hands full trying to drive. Unless the incident results in a traffic accident or assault resulting in injury or death, the victim is often thankful just to get away. Disengaging or separating from the aggressor is the best antidote. But this necessarily requires distance and leaving the scene of the crime. As a result, it's difficult to collect or provide evidence. All of these factors contribute to the underreporting of road rage incidents and frustration for the police as well as victims.

That Laura did have a firearm, a weapon of projection that would make it less likely he would be able to get his hands on her and use his (assumed) superior physical strength, probably gave her additional confidence and helped her to keep calm and formulate a plan. With the gun still in her purse, she nevertheless positioned it on the seat next to her in a manner that exposed the grip for a quick draw. It would have been preferable for the gun to be fixed in a body-mounted holster or one attached to the interior of the car rather than in her purse. This would assure that if the aggressor had driven her off the road and there was a rough ride or a spinout, the gun would not be flung across the interior and out of reach. Being driven off the road might well have disabled her car, and at such point the gun would have been her last means of defense.

In my view, Laura and the aggressive driver were either at two different positions on the continuum or both he and Laura were on two entirely different "tracks" as it were. It wasn't a case when one driver said, "I'll show you" and the other driver said, "No, I'll show you," serving to escalate the aggression. One driver was looking to attack and the other was defending. One displayed emotionally driven acts of aggression but the other did not answer a shove off the road with shoving back. Laura's response to her emotion (fear) was to plan a defense. If the aggressive driver was moving towards the bad end of the continuum, Laura wasn't moving with him and acting recklessly without thought. She set up boundaries ("If he gets beside me like window to window or continued to pursue me I was going to take it out"). She hung in there and watched to see if the boundaries were crossed. If the horn did indeed make the predator's mouth water, he soon learned that while the driver was scared, she wasn't scared enough to give in. This leads us to insights on maintaining enough composure to avoid responding with reckless, competitive actions.

Composure Maintenance Skills

It is important to recognize that emotions such as fear and anger are a product of the reactive mind. But our actions in response to fear and anger are controlled by the cognitive mind. Can you control your actions even when you're afraid or angry? The answer is yes, and most of us do it all the time. For example, think back to the last time you were pulled over for speeding. Did you physically or verbally attack the police officer for ruining your day? No, because you knew it was in your best interest to maintain your composure.

Surviving an attack or assault of any kind begins with implementing "composure maintenance skills."

In an earlier example, we referenced how a professional fighter had lost an important bout because he had "lost his cool." Somehow, the fight had gone beyond his level of composure-maintenance skills. Indeed, one of the traditional reasons why teenagers take up the sport of boxing is that they are always getting into fights at school and in the street. Does boxing in a controlled environment simply help them blow off steam or is there more to it?

Boxing gyms are full of tough kids who formerly got into a lot of trouble. In the gym they are taught sophisticated skills, but more importantly how and when to use them. In the street their fights were powered by raw emotion. Once in training, these same fighters learn to maintain their composure and look for openings to apply their strengths to maximum benefit. For many delinquent youths, being properly coached might be the first time in their lives they've been able to recognize in themselves and appreciate their own ability to learn.

It is important to trust your ability to learn how to maintain your composure. We all have disappointments and stress in our lives. Use these smaller, less-lethal confrontations to practice your composure-maintenance skills. Once you develop the habit of responding immediately with your cognitive mind you will be less likely to meet danger with actions controlled by emotion.

Finally, let's hear from the front lines in public safety. The following insights and tips come not from government or commercial studies but from a panel of road cops, uniformed personnel that spend more time driving on their jobs than just about any other profession. Some of the officers were fine with having their names and departments mentioned and others were restricted or otherwise too modest. My policy was for the vote to be unanimous when it comes to naming names, so we will continue by crediting the following to those who wish only to do their jobs without the need for greater recognition.

Preemptive Behavioral Response to Aggressive Driving and Road Rage

Allow plenty of time.

Take routes that you are familiar with.

Identify possible trouble spots such as sudden merges and short exits.

Avoid U-turns and turning across traffic without the aid of a traffic light.

Choose the lane best suited to your speed.

Choose lanes that avoid merging traffic.

Do not speed or tailgate.

Use the horn only in an emergency.

In Response to Aggressive Driving and Road Rage:

Do not answer any provocation with provocative action of your own.

This includes aggressive maneuvers on your part or hand gestures.

Maintain a wait and watch mindset.

Think of it as an opportunity to practice your composure maintenance skills.

Look for an opportunity to separate.

Use your turn signal and move to the right.

Let them get in front of you.

It is always better to slow down than to get ahead.

Speeding up induces a chase or crash.

If the other person slows down, get on the phone, even if you are just pretending to call 911.

Call 911 and do not hang up no matter what happens, even if you have to put the phone down.

Don't go where you were planning to go.

Find a safe place to go such as:

Police station

Fire station

A well-lit parking lot with plenty of witnesses

Never stop your car.

Chapter 10 The Belligerent Fender Bender

ender bender–type accidents are common and just about every driver is going to suffer collision damage to their cars at one time or another. The cause of the accident could be simple carelessness, minor recklessness, inclement weather, road conditions, or any combination of the above. More often than not, the cause of a fender bender is entirely without malicious intent. Nevertheless, one or both drivers might become irate as the consequences settle in or one driver might come bounding out of their car door ready for a fight. The accident itself may not have been the result of aggressive driving but what if the rage begins after the cars have come to a stop?

It's important to remember that the police are not likely to respond to a crash unless it involves physical injury. This leaves the car owners to manage their own safety. Once the scratching and banging has come to a halt, the first thing you have to do is establish whether or not you or your passengers have been injured. If you are not alone in the car, look each other over for bleeding or abrasions. Make sure everyone is capable of understanding what you are asking and all passengers should be able to provide feedback.

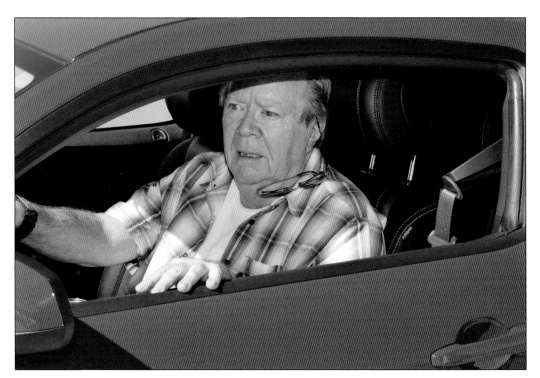

Even a seemingly minor accident can result in the driver or passenger striking their head inside the vehicle. Not only does the gentleman not seem to notice his glasses have been displaced, the look of confusion and lack of recognition could be signs of concussion or a previous medical condition.

After any vehicle incident, whether it was caused by accident or the result of malicious intent, driver and passengers should perform a self-check followed by confirming the status of the people with you (as in a "buddy check"). As seen here, Matthew Brockman of MAST Solutions compares this to condition ACE in a combat situation; A for ammo check and C for casualties. In this case E for equipment check would refer to the drivability of the vehicle.

If you are alone you must perform what is called a self-check.

Feel your body for moisture (bleeding). Press your body parts looking for sore spots. Do you hear a hum or whine indicating hearing loss (which may only be temporary) or concussion. Look at the horizon. Are you dizzy? Are any of your limbs numb? A dull, vibrating pain in the arms or legs may be an indication of fracture.

Just as in a single-car accident, you are going to want to stay inside the car to avoid being hit by oncoming traffic. If the car is in a dangerous position but can be moved, try to do so but avoid positioning your car so that it is blocked in or trapped. Only after you have checked the position of your car and the condition of yourself and your passengers should you check the condition of the driver and occupants of the other vehicle. Again, do so without exiting your vehicle and leave the engine running.

Whether the contact was your fault or not, an argument can ensue. Let them approach you and carefully assess their body language. If they are running towards you and yelling, it's going to be easy to tell they are angry. Less subtle clues are clenching and loosening their fists, lips pressed together, a flushed face, or long determined steps. Remember that there is no way to communicate with, calm down, or work what some call "verbal judo" on an enraged or intoxicated person.

It may take a few minutes for the consequences to sink in and behavior to change for the worse, so remain in your car with the doors locked. Always maintain a

Whenever someone approaches your car with their fists clenched and upper body coiled, that's clear body language that their intent may be to commit violence. A continuation of violence after an aggressive driving or road rage incident is to be expected. But even when a minor collision was indeed an accident, the realization of consequences such as repair costs and insurance rates skyrocketing can cause a sudden shift in behavior. Move your vehicle to safety when necessary but stay in the car until police arrive if summoned. Lower the window just enough to communicate until you are sure it is safe.

physical barrier between yourself and the other driver. Roll down the window only so much as necessary to speak and trade insurance information.

But if the irate "bumpee" or "bumper" is out of control, don't count on any insurance information being offered. Document that you stopped and tried to exchange information but the subject was belligerent or drunk and further interaction could not be done safely. You will need a physical description of the driver as well as date, time, and location. Try to get a cell phone photo of their license plate and if possible a video of their behavior and drive off.

If you have a weapon with you such as a gun, it is important to remember that you cannot brandish, threaten, or try to scare someone off with the gun unless you are trapped and fear for your life.

Responding to a Non-Injury Vehicle Accident

Checklist

Stay in the car with doors locked.

Perform "self-check" for injury.

Move the car if your position is unsafe but do not exit the car.

From inside your car with doors locked observe mood of the other parties.

Watch for telltale signs of aggression.

If the other parties are irate or belligerent:
Photograph or videotape their behavior.

Record their license plate number by photograph if possible.

Use cell phone to call 911 and do not hang up.

If not able to reach 911 operator, pretend you are on the phone with them.

Record the time, date, and place.

Leave the scene if necessary to maintain safety.

Do not brandish a firearm.

Only draw a firearm when you are trapped and in fear for your life.

Chapter 11 Extreme Preparation for Your Vehicle

One could argue that our actions more than anything else have the power to either invite or deter a criminal attack. But that doesn't mean fortifying or "hardening" your vehicle is unnecessary. Just like no one can fully predict the actions of another person, no single protocol or layers of defense can guarantee you will avoid being the victim of violent crime. But there are certain products that can offer greater opportunities for evasion and survival while in your vehicle.

Today, we take for granted many features of the modern automobile and trucks that add security as

Armored cars like this Camaro from D&L Sports, Inc. of Arizona are not only tuned for high performance and able to stop a wide range of incoming fire but also feature strengthening to the bodywork. This enables the car to sustain collision or push another car out of the way without sheet metal collapsing onto the tires. A full armor modification can cost anywhere from $50,000–$100,000 or more. But sensible upgrades such run-flat tires and bulletproof door panels and glass can be added separately for considerably less money. *Photo courtesy of DLSports.com.*

well as comfort. Air conditioning and heat allow you to keep the windows up in any weather with control of all windows from the the driver's seat. (Bear in mind that early automobiles did not have side windows, just wind deflectors in front of the driver to protect the eyes.) And electronic door locks make it possible to secure all the doors instantly. But when we refer to enhancing the defensive capabilities of a vehicle, there are three primary goals. First, to keep the car rolling so escape and/or evasion is possible, second, making the windows and bodywork impenetrable, and third, increasing the likelihood of recovering the car itself and assisting in locating the passengers.

Many consider the tires to be the weakest component of automotive design. But run-flat tires are readily available from a number of makers including Continental, Bridgestone, Michelin, Pirelli, and Goodyear. There are currently two different designs, self-supporting and auxiliary supported. Self-supporting run-flat tires offer a heavier carcass (sidewall and tread) capable of supporting the weight of the vehicle without being inflated. Not indefinitely, mind you, but for a much longer period of time or distance than conventional tires. Auxiliary support tires are able to keep the vehicle rolling not by way of a stiffer tire but by coming to rest on an inner support ring acting as a wheel within the tire.

Self-supporting run-flat tires are available and many new carmakers offer them as optional equipment. Run-flat tires typically offer a harsher ride to one degree or another, weigh more, and negatively affect fuel mileage, but reportedly only by about two percent. But the cost for run-flat tires can be as much as 30 percent higher than conventional tires. They are also not easily repaired.

Auxiliary support tires are more effective in fending off deflation because they do not rely upon the tire itself. Pricing varies but top-of-the-line auxiliary support tires like those from Texas Armoring Company (TAC) located in San Antonio, Texas, are formulated from a high-strength compound designed to resist crack propagation from ballistic attack and severe road hazards.

Texas Armoring Corporation, located in San Antonio, Texas, is one of the premier providers of armored protection for vehicles used by diplomats and VIP security firms the world over. A visit to their 50,000 square foot facility revealed the intensive modification of a variety of vehicles in different stages of construction. *Photo by the author, courtesy of Texas Armoring Corporation.*

Commercially available run-flat tires typically rely upon a rigid carcass to support the vehicle in the event of deflation. Texas Armoring Corporation offers what is in effect a wheel within a wheel that meets U.S. Army, NATO/FINABEL standards for military vehicles. In the event of the tire being completely shredded, this insert should be able to support the vehicle for 50 km at 50 km/hr (or about 30 miles at 30 mph) *Photo by the author, courtesy of Texas Armoring Corporation.*

More than just a solid wheel within the tire, the TAC RCR Runflats are comprised of two components, a roller and a runner designed to "rotate" about the wheel at the same speed as the tire.

This design reduces friction and heat buildup. They are the run-flat choice on all U.S. Government Armored Vehicles. How far can the typical passenger vehicle travel on TAC RCR tires? If an armored vehicle weighing much more than a standard passenger vehicle can meet the U.S. Army, NATO/FINABEL speed and distance standards of 50 km at 50 km/hr (or about 30 miles at 30 mph), the typical passenger car should be that much more secure.

When it comes to the bullet-resistant properties of civilian truck and automobile bodies, there are soft spots and hard spots. While the gears used in crank windows provided some incidental armor, the presence of a motor plus gearing in today's car doors adds even more. To lend a more homogeneous margin of

safety, Kevlar panels can be used to line the doors. They range from soft armor that hangs on the interior side of the doors and can be easily removed, to those that are custom-cut to maintain original appearance. Soft armor including a bomb blanket on the flooring may only add as little as 500 to 600 pounds to the overall weight of the vehicle. But a complete armoring can add two thousand pounds or more, necessitating a complete rework of the suspension.

If strengthening the suspension to support the weight of the armoring and retain controllability when cornering are obvious issues, most people forget that bulletproof glass, especially panels able to deflect rifle ordnance, weighs much more than standard side glass.

This means the actuators, or the mechanism that raises and lowers the windows, must be replaced. This includes the support arm and the motor that drives it.

Soft armoring is not meant to withstand armor piercing rounds or heavy rifle fire, but it does add much less weight to the vehicle (only about 500 pounds including a bomb blanket on the flooring). This should be adequate unless you'll be going up against terrorists or professional kidnappers. One reason why soft armor is less expensive when compared to hard armor is because the lighter weight means that suspension components may need only a minor upgrade. *Photo by the author, courtesy of Texas Armoring Corporation.*

Window glass up to 40mm thick is much heavier than standard window glass. Capable of protecting vehicle occupants from rifle as well as handgun fire, these windows are as hard as granite to the touch. *Photo by the author, courtesy of Texas Armoring Corporation.*

The weight of the extra thick glass (actually a laminate of glass and polycarbonate) requires the installation of an extra heavy-duty actuator to raise and lower the windows. Note the tight, form-fit application of the heavy armor plating that not only can deflect heavy ordnance but is also called upon to support the actuator. *Photo by the author, courtesy of Texas Armoring Corporation.*

Preparation for armoring begins with stripping out all of the wiring, the door panels, trim, and hardware. *Photo by the author, courtesy of Texas Armoring Corporation.*

If you've ever wondered why armoring is so expensive, it's because the work is highly labor intensive. Here the support structure for all the trim and panels has been cut away and set aside. Once the armor plating has been form-fit to the inside of the body shell, the structure to support decorative trim and door panels will be welded back into place. Only a trained eye will be able to distinguish the finished product from the original vehicle. *Photo by the author, courtesy of Texas Armoring Corporation.*

A true armoring build includes not only the most likely surfaces such as doors and windows, but protecting operation components such as the battery box, radiator, fuse boxes, ram bumpers, heavy side panels, and self-sealing fuel tank among other points.

Full armor builds like those offered by TAC treat the passenger compartment as a single unit including the firewall between the engine compartment and the dashboard and the pillars that support the roof. This can cost as much as $185,000 on an existing vehicle. But partial builds that replace the glass, armor the four doors plus the hatch (if applicable) to withstand handgun rounds up to and including .44 Magnum and 12-gauge buckshot will cost about $45,000.

The concept of preparing an automobile for handgun and shotgun fire (referred to as a T4 partial build) fits right in with a scenario wherein a fender bender turns into an argument and one party retrieves a gun and starts firing.

But given that the AR-15 rifle is widely owned, a higher level of protection such as T6 may be necessary even if you are able to drive off. Higher levels of protection are available for heavier weapons but this would also include AR-15 rounds if the ammunition being fired is capable of piercing armor.

For more answers about hardening our vehicles we turned to Dave Lauck, proprietor of D&L Sports in Arizona, who was voted the 2012 Pistolsmith of the

Radiators are a key point of vulnerability and so are electronics. Texas Armoring applies heavy casings that can deflect just about any level of ordnance. *Photo by the author, courtesy of Texas Armoring Corporation.*

Bulletproof glass consists of alternating layers of polycarbonate and glass with the polycarb on the outer skin and the surface facing the interior. Able to deflect the most powerful handgun rounds such as .357 Magnum, this windshield is more than five times as thick as the glass used for standard passenger cars. *Photo by the author, courtesy of Texas Armoring Corporation.*

Glass capable of stopping heavy rifle fire requires additional layers compressed to about 40mm thick, nearly twice the thickness of glass capable of withstanding a .357 Magnum. Here we see the depth of impact illustrated by fracturing of the surface layers, yet the windshield was able to stop the bullets and stay in one piece. *Photo by the author, courtesy of Texas Armoring Corporation.*

Year by the American Pistolsmiths Guild. D&L Sports produces a series of custom defense vehicles. Two- or four-wheel drive high performance and luxury models are available. Lauck is a straight-shooting, no-nonsense type of guy, so we asked him what steps if any could be taken to improve the defensive capabilities of an everyday driver.

According to Lauck, every vehicle should have a "Go Bag." The Go Bag is an emergency kit in the form of a soft-sided bag with shoulder strap so it can be carried hands free.

Inside the go bag should be a knife for cutting a seat belt, stripping clothing in the event wounds must be treated, and obviously for defense. The knife should have a reinforced butt (the tip at the handle end of the knife) for the purpose of breaking glass. It should also include a basic medical kit consisting of tape, wound packing material such as a roll of gauze, and a tourniquet. Celox, a widely available granulated compound that helps blood coagulate quickly, comes in small packages. The primary goal of the medical kit is to stop bleeding. A small squeeze bottle of distilled water for irrigating a wound is a good idea. This will help wash away blood that prevents you from seeing the actual source of the bleeding. Some people like to carry a candy bar simply because blood loss or heightened stress can bring on a diabetic-like crash, leaving the person weak or confused.

The V-Slinger from Vanquest makes an ideal Go Bag. Besides a special compartment for handgun and spare ammunition, it can be loaded with survival tools and medical equipment. This includes a reusable SAM splint, heat-saving blanket, HALO seal for chest-cavity wounds, multiple tools for extrication such as a seat belt cutter, glass breaker, and all manner of wound and bite care. Not to mention MREs (meals ready to eat) or a candy bar that can help stem diabetic crash. The exterior of the bag is covered with MOLLE loops and rigging so additional gear can be easily attached. Note the CPR mask in its blue pouch mounted on the outside of the bag for quick access. I always turn on the little flashlight before putting the bag down so I can relocate it quickly in reduced light.

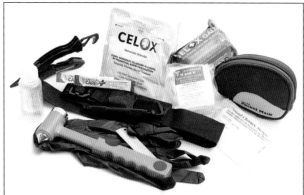

When putting together a "Go Bag" complete with firearms and extra ammunition, don't forget about medical supplies and tools. The tools should be primarily for extrication. Shown here are a multi-tool with seat belt cutter and an impact tool for window breaking. A locking blade can also be swung out from the handle. The medical equipment focuses primarily on stopping blood loss including tourniquet, a supply of gauze for packing wounds, a Celox coagulant powder (hemostatic granules), and wound closure strips. A ten-foot roll of Celox impregnated gauze is also recommended as is a squeeze bottle of wound flushing agent plus a supply of nitrile gloves. It's a good idea to pack the bandage materials torn slightly open. You never know how difficult it may be to open the packaging and you don't want to be struggling when you may not have the strength. Distilled water in a squeeze bottle can serve as a flushing agent, as will contact lens fluid in a pinch. Granulated aspirin is handy for countering the onset of a heart attack. A pocket mask can be used safely on just about any size person, from baby to elderly, and will do the least damage and probably cause less pain to anyone with a facial injury. For liability reasons you may not want to treat a complete stranger but if you get some training beyond first aid, you may be able to maintain a life until the professionals arrive.

Modern Go Bags like the VanQuest VSlinger are an efficient way to conceal guns and ammunition as well as transport medical and survival supplies. The VSlinger's single shoulder strap design allows for the bag to be moved in front of the operator very quickly for complete access without having to remove it. Not only does this provide for a quick draw, no matter how you move, all of the bag's contents stay with you.

You can improvise a Go Bag very easily but there are a number of go bags commercially available that also include a holster and built-in pouches for extra pistol magazines. A secure compartment built into the vehicle for weapons storage can be as elaborate as hidden compartments inside the interior or trunk.

The best access to a firearm while seated in a vehicle is on your person. This means wherever you go, the gun goes with you. Keeping the gun in a go bag next to you on the seat can be hazardous because even a sharp turn in the course of normal driving can move the bag out of reach. There are numerous ways to secure a handgun within reach using a proper holster or simply placing it inside a glove box or console so long as it is protected from loose items that can interfere with attaining a grip or working its way into the trigger guard or other parts of the action.

One of the primary concerns for the average citizen is shots fired into the car during a road-rage incident. Armoring the door panels and adding bullet-resistant glass are probably the most highly-recommended upgrades but adding hard armor to the seats is also a very good idea. Run-flat tires can be a lifesaver on the highway even if your car is never attacked by anything but a road hazard.

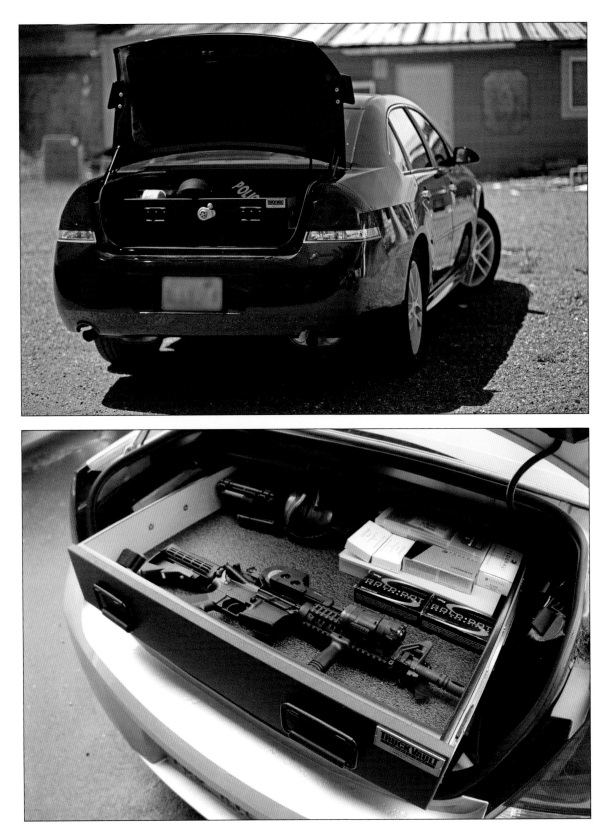

TruckVault leads the way in custom-made lockable compartments for the secure storage of firearms inside of vehicles. Popular with law enforcement personnel, many concerned civilians (as well as hunters) have installed them in sedans as well as pickup trucks and SUVs. *Photo courtesy of TruckVault.*

A fear second only to shots being fired into the car is it becoming disabled as the result of being run off the road. This is actually a more likely scenario than being shot at during a road rage incident. As pointed out in Chapter 9, the number one goal is to separate from the attacker. You can't do this if your car is disabled. The perpetrator of a road rage incident is most likely to implement an impact weapon or firearm when you are trapped in your car, so you want it to be strong enough to absorb some punishment and keep rolling. That's why it's important to install a ram bumper system that reinforces the vehicle from beneath a minor cosmetic change that is in fact designed to enhance the appearance of the vehicle. Not only does this make the vehicle less likely to be disabled as the result of impact, it also increases the vehicle's offensive capability so that precision immobilization techniques (PIT maneuvers) can be performed without damage. A common PIT maneuver is to use the nose of the car to push on the rear quarter panel of another car to spin it out and create an opportunity to escape. Without reinforcement, the likelihood of collapsing the sheet metal into the wheel well of your car and cutting down a tire is increased.

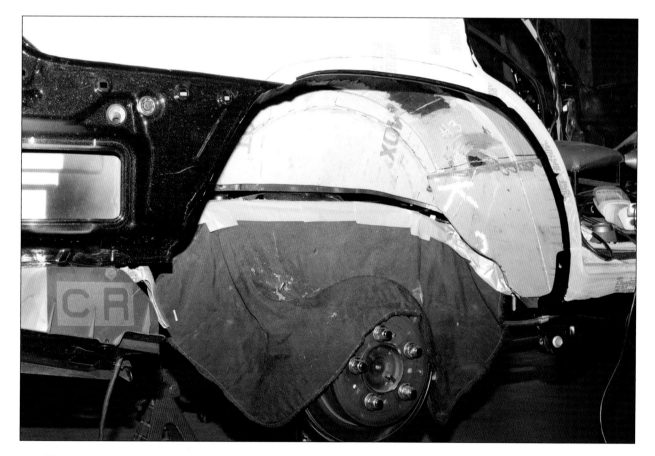

One of the ways in which a vehicle can be rendered immobile is by impact collapsing the wheel well and puncturing the tires. Should the tires lose inflation or be completely shredded from the rims, an inner wheel of nearly indestructible composite material will allow the vehicle to continue. *Photo by the author, courtesy of Texas Armoring Corporation.*

Priorities for Increasing the Defensive Capabilities of Your Vehicle

Run-flat tires

Ensures vehicle control despite tire damage due to road hazard or criminal attack.

Bullet-resistant glass

Stops or significantly slows incoming projectiles in cases of flying debris caused by other vehicles, storm winds, or bullets from small arms fire.

Hard armor door panels

Stops or significantly slows bullets from small arms fire.

Hard armor seats

Stops or significantly slows bullets from small arms fire. Protects against being fired upon from inside the vehicle as in a carjacking or abduction. Provides cover for counterattack.

Hard armor for operational components such as the radiator, battery, and fuses.

Strengthen bumpers and panes surrounding wheels and tires to keep the vehicle from being disabled and unable to escape.

Go Bag

Supplies medical aid, escape tools, and weaponry.

Weapons locker

A small locker in console or otherwise in reach of driver or larger compartment in trunk area to secure weapons when not in the vehicle.

Chapter 12 Terrorist Attacks and the Active Shooter

Terrorist attacks such as those that occurred on September 11, 2001, the 1983 bombing of the United States and French military barracks in Beirut, Lebanon, and the suicide bombing of the USS Cole in 2000 have little in common with an active shooter scenario. But attacks carried out by just a few well-armed shooters upon an unarmed public in Mumbai, India, disarmed military personnel on the grounds of Fort Hood, and employees of the Inland Regional Center in San Bernardino, California, who were likewise prohibited from being armed do in fact resemble both the circumstance and the results of attack by active shooter. Attacks such as these are likely to be repeated again and again simply because the wreaking of terror on the unarmed is literally as easy as "shooting fish in a barrel."

A key element of a successful terrorist attack is surprise. A box cutter with a blade barely larger than a nickel was not viewed as a weapon. Nor were the airliners themselves until they were commandeered and flown off course with two airliners hitting the World Trade Center towers, another slamming into the Pentagon, and another lost over land when a melee broke out between the hijackers and a number of brave passengers. The intentions of a small boat approaching and pulling alongside the Navy Destroyer USS Cole as it was refueling in Yemen were not known. Indeed its presence was the cause of confusion rather than action until it exploded, killing seventeen U.S. sailors and injuring many more. The two bomb-laden trucks used in the Beirut barracks attack delivered the Marine Corp's highest death toll on a single day since World War II. Eighteen American sailors and other members of the Multinational forces were also killed. The trucks served as weapons for a then-obscure group calling itself Islamic Jihad. The element of surprise was key to the success in each of these attacks.

The success of an active shooter also depends on the element of surprise. But more important is one additional characteristic, that of the "soft target." In the case of every mass shooting, oftentimes by a lone gunman, the active shooter has chosen a soft target, meaning people or groups of people that are unarmed. The citizenry of India, even in the teeming capital formerly known as Bombay, are forbidden the possession and use of firearms. The military personnel on base at Fort Hood were forbidden by regulation to carry loaded weapons. It was civilian police, including a female officer who was legally armed, that stopped the attack. The San Bernardino attackers were later killed after they had fled, which is highly unusual in terms of it being classified a terrorist attack.

Howard Safir, the former NYPD and NYFD Commissioner under Mayor Rudolph Giuliani and now Chairman and CEO of Vigilant Resources International (VRI) was probably correct when in a FOX News Channel report aired live the day after the December 2, 2015 attack by Syed Rizwan Farook and Tashfeen Malik in San Bernardino, California, he said that the assault "at least appears to be planned attack, maybe it wasn't planned for yesterday and maybe the dispute at the party caused it to accelerate but certainly this is a group of people who were intent on providing a terrorist incident somewhere."

What made the shootings appear to be workplace violence, i.e., an active shooter(s) incident was that it initially stemmed from an argument at what has been described as an office "holiday" party. The circumstance of the party, which no matter what you call it leans heavily on the celebration of the birth of Jesus Christ and the presence of devout followers including a Messianic Jew, was said to be an irritant. The religious aspect could certainly be considered the first clue that this was a terrorist attack, but when Farook and Malik fled the scene after the slaughter they left behind three pipe bombs. The bombs did not detonate, but the tactic of drawing professional responders to the scene of a killing for the purpose of creating an even bigger event via booby trap is MO right out of the terrorist's playbook. A visit to their home revealed it was for all practical purposes a bomb factory and terrorist enclave.

Safir's assessment was that the arms and ordnance taken to the scene of the party and left behind at their house was probably meant for a bigger attack or even as supplies for a series of attacks. The longer range plans for these weapons were probably short-circuited by the emotions of Farook and Malik that equated to something like, "Oh yeah, you want Jihad—we'll show you Jihad." According to reports attributed to the FBI, Malik was associated with Shabab, the Islamist militant movement in Somalia, and another with the (Al) Nusra Front, the wing of Al Qaeda in Syria. Malik had recently pledged allegiance to Islamic State on Facebook.[1] You have to wonder what their contacts with Al Qaeda and ISIS might have expected from them longer term. Probably something much bigger had been prevented merely because they had lost their cool.

The biggest fear we face is a suicide bomber exploding not just ordnance containing anti-personnel fragmentation such as a pressure cooker filled with nails, but a "dirty" bomb that releases into the atmosphere a disease that is communicable and extremely difficult to defeat medically. Or even a chemical gas or a nuclear weapon. To this end, standing up to such attacks hand-to-hand, in a gang with or without a weapon, is likely to be ineffective. But what about more conventional terrorist attacks such as the shootings at Fort Hood or the Inland Regional Center in San Bernardino?

In the event of an active shooter-style attack on a soft (unarmed) target, escape is the primary goal and should be pursued as the first option. Those that act to escape without hesitation are the people you'll see being interviewed afterwards on the news. Take your family and as many people as you can with you but get out immediately. According to police, if you are not law enforcement (i.e., a sworn officer) you have no moral obligation to engage the attackers or even to help others. If you do so, you will likely be killed.

The first secondary option is to lock down with barricade in a secure area or lock and block.

Lock the doors and windows and cover them with whatever you have available. Create a barricade even if it is just a pile of desks and chairs. Push and stack everything not nailed down against the door. At the very least you must make it not worth the time and effort for the attacker to breach your blockade.

Report to 911. Everyone should be continuing to build the blockade with the least physically able person on the phone with 911, but you still must look for a way to escape. Use a chair or whatever is available to break through a wall. Look for a way to enter the subceiling to hide or escape.

In most cases, the barricade will eventually fail. At this point, the best defense is a good offense. You will likely have to improvise a weapon. Use your imagination. Just about anything you can pick up will fit into one or more of three categories—objects that can be used to strike, puncture, or slash. Heavy objects too difficult to swing can also be dropped for concussive purposes.

Have a plan. Decide among yourselves who is going to strike with the weapon and who is going to wrap them up (subdue them). Which person is going to go high and which one is going to go low? Meaning who is going after the arms and who is going to grab the legs? Who is going to grab the weapon? Is there another person ready with an electric cord to tie them up or will it be a matter of striking until the threat stops?

Having a plan made up of individual assignments assumes that you have a team. Team building for active shooter defense is different than putting together a company volleyball team because winning is not about bragging rights or a trophy. An active shooter incident puts everyone into a do-or-die situation, which brings us to the first ingredient of survival—mindset. Everyone on the team has to be convinced that no matter what has taken place in their lives up until this moment, the actions taken in the next few minutes will determine if they live or die. At this point, you realize that it would have been smart for the office manager to have called a meeting and drilled everyone on a designated plan of action and escape. If only there were a policy of regular active shooter drills just like a mandated fire drill.

The moment you realize that a shooter is on the premises and their perception of your building interior is that of a fish tank and you are the fish might actually be the first time you'll visualize the nearest exit as a means of escape. Or the first time you see a false ceiling as a place to hide, realize that a fire extinguisher can be a weapon, or find the strength to move desks and filing cabinets into position in an effort to block the door. What if you started looking around your office space right now? On a recent visit to the offices of a local business, I was able to make certain observations about the tactical liabilities of the interior layout and generate insights into team building.

The agency was located in a four-story office building elevated above street level to accommodate a parking garage. Access to the first floor was via stairs with an elevator located in the center of the building.

The agency I visited consisted of a string of offices and meeting rooms on the first floor feeding from a main hallway that had one entrance opening directly to the street and three others leading to the central corridor. I suggested that all the doors be locked from the inside and that employees should be issued a key (electronic or otherwise). Visitors or couriers dropping off documents would need to be directed to the correct source, so why not have someone meet them at the door? Security cameras would be a significant upgrade with screens monitored from the reception desk but simply locking the doors for selective entry would probably be the simplest and the most effective approach.

Only a few of the individual office spaces had doors that locked. I recommended either installing dead bolt locks to all doors or a mechanical door jam operated from inside. Office furniture should in position so it can be easily moved to in front of the door.

Most of the meeting rooms had windows facing the hall and most of the doors to the offices had smaller windows along the sides. I would recommend being aware of the lines of sight through each window as this would describe the most vulnerable positions to gunfire. This would also help define positions of concealment. I would also suggest decorative ways to obscure the windows.

All but one of the office doors reached from floor to ceiling. I prefer a standard-height doorway. While a floor-to-ceiling door can be considered a solid barrier, attacking anyone entering the room from over the top of the door can be very effective.

Offices on the perimeter of the building were fit with exterior windows consisting of heavy laminate glass. This glass would likely prove very difficult to break even with the heaviest items typically found in an office space such as a fire extinguisher or a hard drive. As a result, window escape in this environ would be unlikely.

One of my first questions upon meeting the staff was, "Does anyone here have a black belt in Karate

There simply aren't that many secure places to hide inside the typical office. Hiding behind a door can be a losing proposition unless you can reach over the top with a weapon that can project. A handgun offers the most stopping power in this situation but the first shot might be blind so you'd better make sure it's the bad guy behind the door and not someone else trying to escape.

When immediate escape is not possible, blockading is essential. Any resistance to entry means the shooter will have to expend more time without knowing how long they have until first responders arrive. Any time spent banging on one door means less time taking out easier targets, frustrating the active shooter. But your mindset in forming the blockade must take into account that the blockade will likely be breached. Therefore, a plan of counterattack must be formulated. Here the group is huddled away from the windows and on the hinged side of the door. The gentleman is pulling the table against the door to provide greater resistance. Note that he is pulling with his back to the wall rather than pushing against the table from the other side. This position offers greater safety because it is further away from the possible line of fire.

or Jiu-Jitsu?" I then asked, "Is anyone here a Golden Gloves champion? Yes, no? When was the last time you were in the ring and won a quick decisive victory?" The point is that even an elite fighter's skills are perishable. Of the dozen or so employees that were present, only one of them had ever fired a gun of any kind and had little subsequent training.

If everyone in the establishment were armed, then it would just be a matter of taking up a position that provides the most safety from rounds coming their way and shooting the intruder. But any establishment where people are known to be armed or possibly be armed is rarely, if ever, a target for terrorists or an active shooter. I then asked them if they knew what it took for two or more unarmed people to overcome a well-armed active shooter or terrorist. In my view what it takes to overcome them is not

entirely about your individual fighting skill. At least not in the sense you might think about fighting in a one-on-one "put up your dukes" scenario. In this case, the team must assault like a small army unit. Each member of the unit must take an assignment and finish that assignment. In addition, each member of the unit or team must be ready to transition to another assignment depending on the flow of the fight.

Short of a one-shot lucky hit, such as knocking out the shooter with a baseball bat from behind as he passes you in the hall, there are at the very least two primary assignments to fighting an active shooter—trap the weapon with the muzzle facing in the direction so that if the weapon is fired it will not injure you or anyone else, and incapacitate or effectively restrain the shooter.

During the process of building the blockade, make up your mind about what your role will be when the blockade is breached. Think only of your assigned task to block out fear. When the breach has begun, it's difficult to know exactly when to make contact and help the intruder into the trap. But the sooner you can control the direction of the muzzle of the gun, the better. Hold on tight and be prepared to grip harder should the gun go off just as we grit our teeth when we experience pain. Use the shooter's own forward motion to bring him in and expose more of the gun. The object is to trap the weapon and keep the shooter from backing out at all costs. Should the shooter be allowed to move to his rear, you will all be in the direct line of fire.

Everyone in the group formerly huddled in the corner is part of the counterattack. But take note the strongest member of the group is not the one delivering the blow. The decidedly-beefy man is concentrating on locking up the weapon. But instead of relying on grip strength to grab the weapon, he is trapping the gun with his arm wrapped around the weapon with his own hand locking down on his shirt. He appears to be trying to control the shooter's body, but trapping more of the weapon by wrapping his other arm over the weapon and gripping his left wrist would be more secure. The shooter is not going to let go of the weapon so maintaining control of the weapon is imperative. While the shooter is trying to hold on to the gun he is wide open to a blow from an improvised weapon directly to the eye. Objects such as a letter opener or, in this case a screwdriver, are items typically found around the office that can be devastating weapons when directed at highly vulnerable parts of the anatomy, regardless of the operator's strength or ability. A third member of the team could likewise wrap their arms around the shooter's legs at knee level to bring them to the ground. The fourth member of the team can be on the phone with 911 or tasked with tying the shooter up.

A two-person team should consist of someone trapping the weapon and the second person either delivering a blow with a weapon or helping to get the shooter to the ground. In this photo, a belt which could be used to tie up the shooter once on the ground is being use to destabilize. But the act of pulling might cause the lady with the belt to stand up and be in front of the muzzle, putting herself in danger of being shot. A better technique would be to move in and wrap her arms around the shooter's legs behind the knees, causing his legs to buckle.

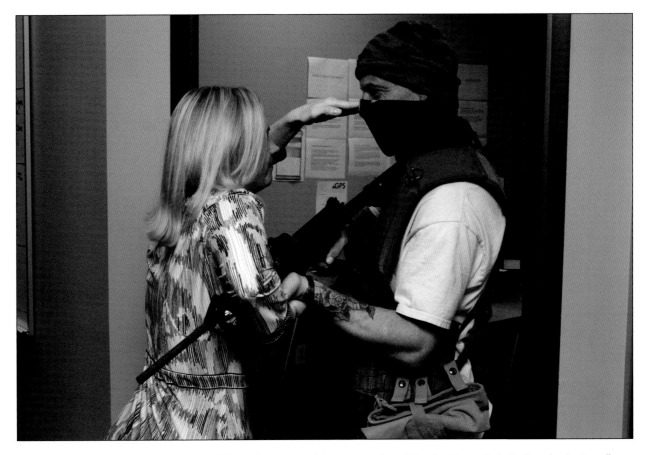

In facing the active shooter one-on-one, it's actually better if you can get right up next to them. Otherwise it is certain death. Since the shooter will likely enter the room leading with the weapon, engaging immediately from the edge of the doorway may be the best option. Pushing the barrel away and trapping the weapon, wrapping it with your arm while striking with a pen, a ruler, or anything that can jab, will be effective if you can strike them in the eyes. Even fingertips will do. Aim for the top of the cheekbone and the funnel of the eye socket will lead you in. Striking to the top of the cheekbone into the eye will also likely bypass any glasses or goggles the shooter may be wearing.

Faced with the gravity of the above assignment, it might be appropriate to once again visit mind-set or more specifically how to deal with fear. Fear releases the gift of adrenaline into our veins, giving us increased strength and sharpening our senses. Fear is thus useful so long as it does not cause us to give in to the impulse to freeze and not fulfill the assignment. The message is to fill your mind with concentration on your assignment so there is no room to worry.

I am sure you have just asked yourself, maybe even said aloud, "What if I am alone?" First of all, escape remains the primary goal. The sooner you can leave the building, the better. A secure hiding place may be the next best choice but it must be fairly sophisticated such as inside a venting system, drop ceiling, or false wall. Hiding beneath a desk or inside a closet is more likely

a trap than a place to hide safely. If you cannot leave nor effectively hide, barricading your position becomes all the more important. Block the door with the heaviest item you can move. If you cannot pick up a desk or filing cabinet, it's important to remember that you may be able to slide it by pushing against it at a point below its center line. Stack anything you can against the door. If the shooter has trouble opening the door he may only open it enough to look in and see only one side of the room so whatever position you take it should be to the hinged side of the door. Or, he may be discouraged altogether as time is not on his or her side. The longer he lingers, the better chance he has of being confronted by first responders.

The object of barricading is first to block entry but it can also provide a moment of distraction that can

The melee in open space shown here brings to light the importance of situational awareness, transition, and control. Let's assume the plan among the three office personnel was for the man to trap the shooter's AR-15 and the lady with the bottle was to strike the shooter while the blonde woman contacted 911. The man in the plaid shirt has successfully trapped the shooter's carbine. In response, the shooter then released his right hand from gripping the weapon. It is absolutely critical that you recognize that any time an active shooter is willing to let go of his weapon by either hand, that hand is about to draw a secondary weapon. In this case it's the black plastic training knife. The woman in the light colored dress reacted by transitioning from her assignment of providing communication to that of trying to control the hand with the knife long enough to create an opening for the striker to land a series of blows with the bottle.

be capitalized on. You may be alone but the strategic advantage of surprise does not require a lot of people. The sound of chairs and boxes, etc. screeching or crashing out of the way may or may not be a surprise to an active shooter. Keep in mind that any extra effort in opening the door means less physical effort is being devoted to supporting his rifle, shotgun, or pistol. This could create an opportunity to gain an advantage.

The active shooter is likely to enter the room with the muzzle of the gun leading the way. Grabbing and redirecting the barrel of the gun may be one possibility but the other hand must present a weapon. Grabbing it with one hand and striking with a pen, ruler, or anything that can jab will be effective if you can strike them in the eyes. Even fingertips will do. Aim for the top of the cheekbone

and the funnel of the eye socket will lead you in. Striking to the top of the cheekbone into the eye will also likely bypass any glasses or goggles the shooter may be wearing.

The team approach to barricade, trap, and overcome can be difficult to replicate by a single person. But there is really no alternative if you are discovered. If you have the ability to decorate your office space, start planning now. Every desk should have a heavy paperweight and a letter opener. A plant with heavy pot is good for barricading and so are filing cabinets that can be moved independently. Keep a couple of doorstops in your desk and an aerosol can of bug spray or oven cleaner. If you can deflect the weapon long enough to spray their eyes, you have a good chance of surviving. When you begin with the

Trapping the weapon so that the any wild shot will not hit you or anyone else not only offers protection but also causes the active shooter to fight for the gun, leaving him open to being hit, cut, taken down, or choked. The lady pushing down and away on the weapon is grimacing but the personnel in these photos are not actors but members of the office staff. That she is injecting emotion into a staged scene with deactivated weaponry is valuable because she is visualizing the struggle, imagining herself holding on to the gun even tighter should the gun go off.

premise that anyone can be ambushed, it shouldn't be difficult to imagine yourself prevailing against just about anyone.

There may be more attackers so overcoming one attacker means that you should either attempt an escape to the outside of the building or reset the barricade and prepare to repeat the process of attacking the attacker. Be prepared to implement this over and over until contacted by first responders.

Options for Surviving an Active Shooter–Style Event

Preparation for Active Shooter Events

Know where all the exits are.

Designate alternative escape routes:
   Windows
   Thin walls
   Ventilation systems

Recognize which furniture or other objects can be used to barricade.
  Suggest additional furnishing, floor mounted plants, etc.
Improvise weapons:
  Furnish desk with letter opener and heavy paperweight.
  Keep a screwdriver and hammer in a desk drawer.
  Keep an aerosol can of bug spray or oven cleaner.
Visualize an ambush style plan of action based on halls and doorways.

During an Active Shooter Event

Escape.
Lock down and barricade.
Continue to look for escape route.
  Consider breaking through walls, ceilings, or windows.
Report to 911.
Plan an offense for when your barricade is breached.
  Use improvised weapons.

  Designate tasks:
    Who will strike, puncture, slash, etc.?
    Who will immobilize arms or legs?
    Who will go for the active shooter's weapon?
Once one active shooter is apprehended or subdued, prepare for the next active shooter.
Report to 911.

Escape or:
Refortify barricade and debrief.
  Restock or reload weapons.
  Provide honest feedback.
  Analyze how the defense worked/didn't work.
Reset and prepare offense for when your barricade is breached again.
Continue to look for escape route.
Report your progress to 911.

Addendum: Firearms and the Psychological Edge

Both the terrorist strike and the active shooter are looking to kill the maximum number of victims with the smallest probability of meeting resistance. The ability to scare and strike terror into their victims is based primarily on drawing from their victim's sense of hopelessness, making it clear that their survival is strictly in the hands of the attacker, with no means of stopping the attack in reach. To ensure the maximum amount of terror the active shooter/terrorist invariably picks a soft target, meaning a business, a school or any other type of facility where the possession of a firearm is forbidden or punishable by law. The "gun-free zone" is what encourages the active shooter/terrorist to complete his mission.

Conversely, any area where people are likely to be armed does not extend a psychological comfort zone to a prospective active shooter or terrorist. It is well-known that James Holmes, the shooter who murdered twelve people and injured fifty-eight others in the Century 16 movie theatre in Aurora, Colorado, bypassed other movie houses because they recognized the rights of citizens licensed to carry concealed handguns. The management of the theatre where the slaughter occurred somehow arrived at the conclusion that patrons would be more comfortable if no one was allowed to legally carry a concealed handgun. Of course, this ignores the fact that if a gun were concealed they wouldn't know it was there (being carried legally or otherwise). All the prohibition did was draw the attention of Holmes and accommodate his intentions by offering a very real comfort zone for him to carry out his plan.

Nadal Hassan, the perpetrator of the Fort Hood shooting, was a member of the United States Army stationed there. Aware of the regulations that rendered the soldiers helpless, he knew from the start there would be little if any possible resistance. If the soldiers had been permitted to carry their weapons in at least a preliminary state of readiness (such as loaded magazine inserted into the weapon but chamber empty) the comfort zone would be in favor of the soldiers, destroying the actual advantage, and awarding the psychological edge to the would-be victims of the active shooter.

Avoid being a victim of the Active Shooter

Checklist

Do not patronize businesses that prohibit the private citizen from carrying a firearm.

Do not work in a facility that prohibits the private citizen from carrying a firearm.

Do not elect officials that promote legislation that prohibits the private citizen from carrying a firearm.

Join the NRA and state or local groups that support the right of private citizens to keep and bear arms.

Join local groups and initiatives that promote the legal right to keep and bear arms, especially in theatres, schools, shopping areas, and small businesses.

Support the incarceration of career criminals.

Work with national, state, or local groups that seek to refine and reduce the treatment of at-risk patients with psychotropic drugs.

Appendix A How to Watch Your Back: A Quick Reference Guide to Preventive Measures

Chapter 1: Understanding Preemptive Behavioral Response

Integrate safe actions that reduce vulnerability into your routine to the point at which they become habit:

- Lock doors
- Set alarms
- Look at surroundings before closing doors behind you
- Watch for who is watching you

Integrate tools and weapons into what you wear or take with you every day:

- Keys
- Communication device (cell phone)
- Small flashlight
- Small knife
- "Pepper" spray
- Access to a firearm

Chapter 2: What Everyone Can Learn From the Dangers of Selling Real Estate

Understand the inherent dangers of your job.

How well do you know your clientele?

How does your location or the locations you visit put you at risk?

When shopping for a home or business location:

Do any of the doors and windows display damage that would indicate a break-in?

If the property is vacant, is it secure enough to prevent squatters?

If your marketing includes a personal photograph does the image key on your professional image or is it overly glamorous or egocentric?

All first meetings should occur at the office.

All customers must sign in and be identified.

Confirm the identity of clientele before showing property at a remote location or demonstrating a vehicle for sale.

Does the person's name come up in a simple "Google" search?

Can you access a criminal database?

Is the driver's license or other ID genuine?

Be familiar with what a driver's license from other states should look like.

Use a "blue" light to check for embedded holograms or words that were deleted.

Does the license or other ID appear to be poorly laminated?

Does the person match the description on the ID in the picture and in terms of height, weight, eye color or use of prescription lenses?

Sales agents that leave the premises with customers should be required to check in.

Every agent should have a buddy that will call them at a prearranged time.

All agents should use common language to indicate distress, such as referring to them by a wrong name or mentioning a color code.

Valid confirmed and recorded identification is required for all showings.

All showings should be of a prearranged duration.

Company vehicles or personal vehicles regularly used to show property or make sales calls should have tracking devices.

Don't let a customer get between yourself and an exit.

When showing property the sales person should not enter walk-in closets, basements, garages, or any space that is not well lit. Ask the client if they would like to go inside and wait outside by the door.

Every sales person should be instructed to leave a client or any location any time they feel unsafe.

Do not consume alcohol or drugs (legal or otherwise) with a customer.

Do not accept previously opened water or soda bottles or cans from a customer.

Chapter 3: Fuel Stops—The Great Equalizer

Before choosing a pump, circle the station to see who is watching you.

If your arrival brings undue attention, leave.

Keep your windows rolled up.

Unlock only the driver's side door.

Do not use a pump near or opposite to a car that is parked at the pump but not in the process of filling the tank.

Do not park near or opposite to a car that is parked inordinately distant from the pump. This is a method used for smash-and-grab and "sliders."

When you finally park, wait five seconds.

Use this time to check all the mirrors and look for anyone that is watching you or beginning to approach.

When you first exit the car, stand between the open car door and the driver's seat and look around before heading to the pump.

Check the credit card reader for a skimmer.

The credit card slot should be narrow and clean.

Look for damage to the outer plate surrounding the card reader.

Is there security tape or a seal surrounding the outer plate of the card reader?

Is the tape or seal broken?

Is the security tape or seal double-layered?

Do not use any pump that looks scratched, dented, or shows signs of pry marks.

Do not use a debit card at the pump that requires a Personal Identification (PIN) number. Small cameras can be used to collect PIN numbers.

Modern credit cards can be scanned without being touched. Do not allow anyone to pass near you as you are using a credit card.

Be prepared to answer three or more questions by the card reader.

Don't get caught staring at the screen tuning out everything around you.

Keep your head on a swivel and casually look around after each prompt.

If you intend to walk around the car to inspect the tires, step away from the car and make wide turns at each corner.

Chapter 4: What Everyone Can Learn From Professional Drivers

How to avoid being a victim of smash-and-grab or "Jugging":

Avoid making extra stops after banking or making large purchases.

If your errands include a long list of stops, prioritize so that you go directly home after visiting a bank or buying a "big ticket" item such as a computer or television set.

How to avoid being a victim of a driveway robbery:

Signaling and looking left and right are natural protocol before turning into your neighborhood.

Also check the rearview mirror to see if any car turns in with you.

If you do not recognize the car behind you as you enter the neighborhood or approach your residence, keep driving.

Do not brake suddenly or do anything to acknowledge the other driver.

Leave the neighborhood as though you forgot something at the store.

If they continue to follow, dial 911 and stay on the line with the operator.

Maintain the basic safety features of your vehicle.

Make sure the remote door-locking feature of your vehicle is operating.

Build the habit of locking the doors as soon as you enter.

Do not use the switch to unlock all the doors if you are the only person exiting the vehicle.

If your door locks can be programmed:

Continue to utilize the habit of locking the doors as soon as you enter.

Program the doors to lock when the vehicle is put into gear.

Avoid programming the doors to unlock when the vehicle is put into park.

Maintain the heat and air conditioning units so that the windows do not need to be left in the open position.

Be in control of where you park:

Wherever you go, the presence of anyone that makes you feel uncomfortable in any way is justification for you to leave.

Park with the front of the vehicle facing forward.

Backing out is not only slower but more dangerous.

Backing out limits visibility of both oncoming traffic or an approaching threat.

Always park beneath a light if it is night time or if there is the possibility you may not be returning to the car before dark.

Park as close as you can to the door of your destination as possible.

If you cannot park nearby to your destination try to park in view of or in line with the front door.

If you are visiting a restaurant, sit where you can see the vehicle.

Parking away from a group of cars will allow you to see around the vehicle as you approach.

Do not immediately exit the vehicle after coming to a stop.

Check the rearview, left side, and right side mirrors before opening the doors.

Do not pick up hitchhikers.

Do not open the door or open the window to speak with strangers.

Chapter 5: The Dangers of Drive-Up/Drive-Through Services

Consider the location of the stores and banks that you frequent.
Ask yourself:

Does it also sell liquor or cigarettes?

Is it adjacent to a business that sells liquor or cigarettes?

Drive through the parking area and take notice of who is in attendance.

Ask yourself:

Is anyone waiting around for no apparent reason?

Is anyone in the area dressed inappropriately such as covering their face or wearing heavy clothes on a warm day, sunglasses on a cloudy day, etc.?

Is there a car parked nearby with a driver inside waiting for no apparent reason?

What structures could be used to hide behind?

If you were playing hide and seek where would you hide?

When you park your car turn off the engine, lock the doors, and take your keys.

Do not leave a child unattended in the car.

When on line for service from inside your car, stay far enough behind the car in front of you so that you can see the rear wheels. This will allow you to maneuver out of line.

At the Bank:

Do not use an ATM for making a deposit or checking a balance.

No matter your purpose or intention, in the eyes of criminal your presence at the ATM will always signal a cash withdrawal.

When visiting a bank lobby:

Are the tellers behind bullet-resistant glass?

If not, the bank is more attractive to robbery than other banks that are more secure.

Do not use a walk-up ATM.

Before driving up to an ATM, circle the facility and look for anyone that is on foot or waiting inside a parked car.

If you are in line for the ATM, stay back from the car in front of you so that you can maneuver quickly out of line.

Have your card out and ready before reaching the ATM.

Pull in the side mirror so you can get as close as possible to the slots and keypad without damaging your car.

Look around.

Leaving your car in gear with a foot on the brake is a double-edged sword. If there are pedestrians in the area, leaving in a panic may result in hitting an innocent passerby.

Check the condition of the ATM. If it looks roughed up, a pirate card reader may have been installed.

If there is an inspection sticker that is too obvious or does not appear genuine, a pirate card reader may have been installed.

If the transaction does not go through for any reason, check your balance as soon as possible to see if your data has been compromised.

After you swipe your card, place it inside the car but do not take the time or attention to return it to your wallet or purse at this time.

Look around.

It's natural to want to count the money dispensed by the machines but an ATM, especially one connected directly to a bank, are highly accurate and regulated. In the event of any irregularity the only people that can help are inside the bank or on the telephone so drive off as soon as you have the money and/or receipt in your hands.

Drive off in a direction that offers the least resistance. Choose a path that keeps you moving and allows you to exit to the street quickly.

If you are picking up a prescription at a drugstore that also sells all manner of dry goods, make sure to ask for a bag used for general merchandise. A white paper bag typically used to hold prescription drugs can attract the wrong attention.

If you are going to use a vending machine located on the exterior of a business exposed to the parking lot, choose only the busier hours to do so. No one should be standing or sitting around waiting.

Take someone with you to watch your back while you manipulate the machine and make your choices.

Remain vigilant and demonstrate body language bordering on arrogance that indicates awareness of your surroundings.

Chapter 6: How Safety Plays a Part in Choosing a Handgun for Personal Defense
Hand Positions for Safe Handling as per Design

Single-Action Revolver

Index finger of strong hand outside the trigger guard.

Strong hand thumb resting atop the hammer spur with hammer down.

Note: hammer in down position over a loaded chamber ONLY if the revolver is equipped with a firing pin safety, or transfer bar safety.

Never holster or otherwise carry a single-action revolver with the hammer back.

Double-Action Revolver

Index finger of strong hand outside the trigger guard riding against the exterior of the cylinder.

Strong hand thumb resting atop the hammer spur with hammer down.

Note: older models of double-action revolver that feature a "nose pin" (firing pin mounted directly on the hammer) should not be carried with a loaded chamber beneath the hammer.

Never holster or otherwise carry a double-action revolver with the hammer back.

If the double-action revolver operates with its hammer not visible but enclosed by the frame (sometimes called "hammerless"), be sure to ride the index finger alongside the exterior of the cylinder.

If the hammer is shrouded, place the strong hand thumb on the small but exposed portion of the hammer spur.

If the hammer spur has been reduced or removed altogether, place the strong hand thumb on the outer contour of hammer or the remnant of the hammer spur.

Double-Action Only and Traditional Double-Action (TDA) Semiautomatic Pistols

Index finger of strong hand outside the trigger guard, preferably above the trigger guard and alongside the frame.

Strong hand thumb resting atop the hammer spur with hammer down.

Monitor any movement of the hammer and slide.

Never holster or otherwise carry a TDA pistol with the hammer back unless a mechanical safety is applied.

If the gun is equipped with a mechanical decocker, always use it to lower the hammer before holstering or whenever the sights of the gun are off target.

If a gun requires manual decocking from single-action mode and does not have a working mechanical safety, this is a poor choice of weaponry in my opinion and should be disposed of.

If a gun requires manual decocking from single-action mode and does have a working manual safety, put the gun on safe at the conclusion of fire. Move to a position where a fired round will be safely blocked and absorbed without ricochet before attempting to lower the hammer manually.

Browning 1911 Action Semiautomatic Pistol

Index finger of strong hand outside the trigger guard, preferably above the trigger guard and alongside the frame.

Strong hand thumb rides beneath the platform of the thumb safety.

Upward pressure is applied to the underside of the thumb safety to prevent it from rotating downward to "off-safe" ready to fire.

Striker-Fired Semiautomatic Pistol
Index finger of strong hand outside the trigger guard, preferably above the trigger guard and alongside the frame.
Strong hand thumb resting atop the back of the slide.
Monitor for movement of the slide.

Chapter 7: Handgun Accuracy as a Component of Safety

Hand Position for More Accurate Shooting
A high grip on the handgun offers more control over every aspect of shooting.
Choose a gun that allows you to hold the grip with the least amount of distance from the top of the hand to the bore axis (the center of the barrel).
A high grip allows the trigger finger to move with less deviation.
The greater the angle at which the trigger finger drops to the face of the trigger, the easier it will be to press the finger in a straight line.
Remember:

Only accurate shots on a verified threat will end aggression without putting others in danger.

Chapter 8: Safe Handling Practices in Awkward Situations

Never separate a gun from its holster outside of your home or automobile.
Exception:

Should it become necessary to remove a gun from a holster in a bathroom (public or private), place the gun immediately in a shoulder bag, purse, or briefcase.
Hang the bag on the inside of the stall door or on the door handle on the interior side of the bathroom exit.
Do not place a bag or briefcase containing a gun in a shopping cart.

If you must leave a gun inside your vehicle temporarily:

Create a designated position inside your car for temporary concealed storage of your handgun.
Adapt a lockable compartment within reach of the driver's seat.
Make sure any storage compartment is free of loose items that can travel inside the trigger guard.
Make sure any storage compartment is clean and free of small items that can enter into the action of the firearm.
Position the firearm so it is accessible via a secure finger-off-trigger pre-shooting grip.

When reholstering or rebagging while seated inside a vehicle:

Check to see if the holster or bag is clear before picking up the handgun.

Attain a safe grip with index finger outside the trigger guard.

Look the gun all the way into the holster, whether the holster is belt-mounted or inside a dedicated carry compartment.

When seated in a vehicle with a holstered gun, make sure your clothing does not bind or otherwise hinder a direct path to the gun.

Chapter 9: Commuting and the Road Rage Phenomena

Preemptive Behavioral Response to Aggressive Driving and Road Rage:

Allow plenty of time.

Take routes you are familiar with.

Identify possible trouble spots such as sudden merges and short exits.

Avoid U-turns and turning across traffic without the aid of a traffic light.

Choose the lane best suited to your speed.

Choose lanes that avoid merging traffic.

Do not speed or tailgate.

Use the horn only in an emergency.

In Response to Aggressive Driving and Road Rage:

Do not answer any provocation with provocative action of your own.

This includes aggressive maneuvers on your part or hand gestures.

Maintain a wait and watch mindset.

Think of it as an opportunity to practice your composure maintenance skills.

Look for an opportunity to separate.

Use your turn signal and move to the right.

Let them get in front of you.

It is always better to slow down than to get ahead.

Speeding up induces a chase or crash.

If the other person slows down, get on the phone, even if you are just pretending to call 911.

Call 911 and do not hang up no matter what happens, even if you have to put the phone down.

Don't go where you were planning to go.

Find a safe place to go such as:

- Police station
- Fire station
- A well-lit parking lot with plenty of witnesses

Never stop your car.

Chapter 10: The Belligerent Fender Bender

In response to non-injury vehicle accident:

Stay in the car with doors locked.
Perform "self-check" for injury.
Move the car if your position is unsafe but do not exit the car.
From inside your car with doors locked, observe mood of the other parties.
Watch for telltale signs of aggression.

If the other parties are irate or belligerent:

Photograph or videotape their behavior.
Record their license plate number by photograph if possible.
Use cell phone to call 911 and do not hang up.
If not able to reach 911 operator, pretend you are on the phone with them.
Record the time, date, and place.
Leave the scene if necessary to maintain safety.
Do not brandish a firearm.
Only draw a firearm when you are trapped and in fear for your life.

Chapter 11: Extreme Preparation for Your Vehicle

Priorities for Increasing the Defensive Capabilities of Your Car or Truck:

Run-flat tires:

Ensures vehicle control despite tire damage due to road hazard or criminal attack.

Bullet-resistant glass:

Stops or significantly slows incoming projectiles in cases of flying debris caused by other vehicles, storm winds, or bullets from small arms fire.

Hard armor door panels:

Stops or significantly slows bullets from small arms fire.

Hard armor seats:

Stops or significantly slows bullets from small arms fire. Protects against being fired upon from inside the vehicle as in a carjacking or abduction. Provides cover for counterattack.
Hard armor operational components such as the radiator, battery, and fuses.
Strengthen bumpers and panes surrounding wheels and tires to keep the vehicle from being disabled and unable to escape.

Go Bag:

Supplies medical aid, escape tools, and weaponry.

Weapons locker:

A small locker in console or otherwise in reach of driver, or larger compartment in trunk area to secure weapons when not in the vehicle.

Chapter 12: Terrorist Attacks and the Active Shooter

Preparation for Active Shooter Events:

Know where all the exits are.

Designate alternative escape routes:

Windows.
Thin walls.
Ventilation systems.
Recognize which furniture or other objects can be used to barricade.
Suggest additional furnishings, floor mounted plants, etc.

Improvise weapons:

Furnish desk with letter opener and heavy paperweight.
Keep a screwdriver and hammer in a desk drawer.
Keep an aerosol can of bug spray or oven cleaner.
Visualize an ambush-style plan of action based on halls and doorways.

During an Active Shooter Event:

Escape.
Lock down and barricade.
Continue to look for escape route.
Consider breaking through walls, ceilings, or windows.
Report to 911.

Plan an offense for when your barricade is breached:

Use improvised weapons.

Designate tasks:

Who will strike, puncture, slash, etc.
Who will immobilize arms or legs.
Who will go for the active shooter's weapon.
Once one active shooter is apprehended or subdued, prepare for the next active shooter.
Report to 911.

Escape or:

Refortify barricade and debrief.

Restock or reload weapons.

Provide honest feedback.

Analyze how the defense worked/didn't work.

Reset and prepare offense for when your barricade is breached again.

Continue to look for escape route.

Report your progress to 911.

Avoid being a victim of the Active Shooter:

Do not patronize businesses that prohibit the private citizen from carrying a firearm.

Do not work in a facility that prohibits the private citizen from carrying a firearm.

Do not elect officials that promote legislation that prohibits the private citizen from carrying a firearm.

Join the NRA and state or local groups that support the right of private citizens to keep and bear arms.

Join local groups and initiatives that promote the legal right to keep and bear arms, especially in theatres, schools, shopping areas, and small businesses.

Support the incarceration of career criminals.

Work with national, state, or local groups that seek to refine and reduce the treatment of at-risk patients with psychotropic drugs.

Appendix B Principles of Everyday Survival

Principle 1

There is no freedom without safety.

Principle 2

The one who waits sees more.
Always take time to scan. This is a form of waiting.

Principle 3

Patience equals waiting.
Waiting equals spare time to be used to make a plan.

Principle 4

The five second rule:

One second devoted to scanning each of four corners from the inside of the car or the available field of vision.
The additional or fifth second is for composure.

Principle 5

Strangers are strangers no matter how much they remind you of someone you know.
Strangers are unpredictable.
Humans tend to seek bonding. (More so non-predatory humans.)
The ability to empathize is a key characteristic of healthy human beings.
The ability to reserve empathy for those that are proven to be worthy of it is key to not falling prey.

Principle 6

Head on a swivel:

Keep scanning your field of vision.
Enhance your peripheral vision by turning your head and swiveling at the hip.
Know what you are seeing but don't stare.

Principle 7

Preemptive Behavior and Internal Security Protocol:

Habitually perform routine actions, such as locking your car door and putting on a seat belt, until they become automatic. Building such habits is commonly referred to as preemptive behaviors, which becomes part of your Internal Security Protocol. Think of your Internal Security Protocol as a wall around a castle. The more preemptive behaviors you have in place, the higher and less impenetrable the wall becomes.

Principle 8

Pacing or Punctuation:

Pacing is a method of balancing out moments of distraction or intense concentration with moments of surveillance. For every period of distraction or moment in which you are devoting complete concentration on the chore at hand, there should also be a corresponding period of looking around resulting in genuine recognition of what is before you.

The outward appearance of someone who is punctuating or pacing themselves with moments of surveillance should project an attitude bordering on arrogance, thus offering a higher state of awareness to onlookers as a warning.

Principle 9

Recognition:

Recognition could be finding exactly what you are looking for or not finding what you are looking for. As in, if no one is immediately visible, focus in on positions where someone would hide.

Principle 10

Behind the curve:

Behind the curve means one person has begun their plan of action first. For example, in drag racing it's not unusual for two cars to have the same elapsed time from start to finish. But the first car to leave the starting line will be the winner simply because they moved off the starting line first.

Principle 11

Action beats reaction:

Action beats reaction is closely related to behind the curve. Let's say some loudmouth has already cursed you out and announced he is going to harm you. You have weapons of your own concealed on your person but so far it's just words and there is no imminent danger. Suddenly, the bad guy draws a knife and start towards you. Even though you were informed of the threat and ready to act, your opponent already has his weapon in hand and put his plan into motion. Even if your weapon acquisition takes exactly the same amount of time as your opponent, you are clearly in more danger. If someone starts towards you with a weapon before you even realized there was a threat, that's being behind the curve.

Principle 12

Preventive maintenance of preemptive behaviors and your Internal Security Protocol:

The only way to make sure that a preemptive behavior remains automatic is to be consistent. Standard Operating Procedures, or SOPs, such as wearing a seat belt can only be relied upon to protect if you use them habitually. For example, it might seem unnecessary to buckle your seat belt when just driving down the block to get the mail. But every time you do not use the seat belt you are untraining yourself and degrading an important safety device.

Principle 13

Split objectivity and the internal referee:

One side of the mind is free to be creative, imagining only positive results. The other side of the mind should remain skeptical and vigilant. This mirrors the child/adult mindset of total freedom without regard to consequences versus the responsibility of dealing with negative results. Split objectivity requires an internal referee with the instinct for survival.

Principle 14

Color-coded threat levels:

Grading of threat levels to describe awareness, state of mind, and how it relates to readiness and the will to act. The white state of mind remains unaware and uncaring of any threat or possibility of threat. The yellow state of mind recognizes the constant possibility of threat and is open to taking action when necessary. The orange state of mind recognizes imminent threat and acts to avoid or makes ready for the fight. The red state of mind takes aggressive action in the midst of battle to end the fight.

Instruct friends and family members to refer to color-coded warnings for instant communication. Working a color code into a conversation can be useful in relaying information when the wrong person (i.e., the threat) is listening.

Principle 15

Don't get trapped in the cocoon:

Any chore being performed requires a certain level of concentration. For example, if you are reading a book, your attention can block out anything happening outside of the space between your eyes and the page you are reading. In a store, there are many things happening around you beyond the shelves you are searching. Periodically break out of the cocoon formed by your sightline as you work.

Principle 16

Tethering:

Somewhat specific to property sales or walking into confined spaces. When showing property for sale or otherwise walking with strangers you need not always lead. Let them enter the room but remain by the doorway as they spread out into the space. Tether yourself nearest to a path of escape.

Principle 17

Composure Maintenance Drills:

Any time you come face to face with a frustration, even something so simple as waiting on line, consciously use it as an opportunity to develop your capacity for patience.

Patience is like a muscle you can develop.

Patience allows you to analyze and develop a plan:

Before a confrontation.

During actual combat.

Principle 18

Combat breathing:

The body can be calmed and the mind refocused by practicing a pattern of breathing outlined by US Army Ranger Lieutenant Colonel David Grossman's book *On Combat: The Psychology and Physiology of Deadly Conflict in War and Peace*. The method consists of a repetition of breath in the following manner. Intake through the nose, hold for four seconds, release through the lips to the count of four seconds, and repeat.

Principle 19

Chored focus:

Chored focus is putting aside the enormity and fear of not reaching a complex goal in order to complete a simple technique that is necessary for success. In the most benign circumstance, this could mean a musician playing through pages of boring exercises every day in order to master the instrument. In terms of personal defense, chored focus serves to distract your mind from whatever quantity of fear is in danger of rendering you inactive. For example, to prevent an active shooter from entering your room, the first chore is to barricade the door. To barricade the door you must move a filing cabinet but it's too heavy to lift. Sitting on the floor with your back against the cabinet you discover it will slide when pressure is applied below its centerline. You forget about everything else but the chore of pushing off with your legs until the cabinet stops against the door.

NOTES

Chapter 1

1. "Presidential Initiative for Increasing Seat Belt Use Nationwide," http://ntl.bts.gov/data/letter_nz/seatbelt .pdf; America's Experience with Seat Belt and Child Seat Use, http://www.nhtsa.gov/people/injury/airbags/ Archive-04/PresBelt/america_seatbelt.html
2. Cynthia Block Reid, "Historic Trauma Cases: Dale Earnhardt," http://nursing.advanceweb.com/Artile/Historic-Trauma-Cases-Dale-Earnhardt.aspx
3. Brian Enos, *Practical Shooting: Beyond Fundamentals* (Clifton, Colorado: Zediker Publishing, 1990), 139.
4. George H. S. Singer, Joanne Singer, Robert H. Horner, "Using Pretask Requests to Increase the Probability of Compliance for Students with Severe Disabilities," *Research and Practice for Persons With Severe Disabilities,* December 1987 12: 287-291, http://rps.sagepub.com/content/12/4/287.full.pdf+html
5. S. Englemann and G. T. Colvin, (1983) Generalized compliance training. Austin TX: Pro-Ed.
6. Nakia Cooper, "Police Say Man Who Murdered Elderly Sharpstown Woman was 'Crazy, Demented," www .click2houston.com, May 7, 2005, http://www.click2houston.com/news/suspect-arrested-in-fatal-stabbing-of-79yearold-elderly-woman/32812256

Chapter 2

1. Jay MacDonald, "ID Thieves Target Home Equity Lines," Bankrate.com, Nov. 14, 2008, http://www .bankrate.com/finance/home-equity/id-thieves-target-home-equity-lines-1.aspx
2. Ben Lane, "Real Estate Agent Narrowly Escapes Kidnapping by Registered Sex Offender," housingwire .com, Jan. 12, 2015, http://www.housingwire.com/articles/32575-real-estate-agent-narrowly-escapes-kidnapping-by-registered-sex-offender
3. Associated Press, "Real Estate Agent Killed, Tenant Arrested," Oct. 2, 2008, http://www.wtvy.com/news/ georgia/headlines/30168624.html
4. https://www.youtube.com/watch?v=oOrMu7VHGZ8
5. "Fallout from the murder of real estate agent Beverly Carter," foxnews.com, Oct. 2, 2014, http://video .foxnews.com/v/3817218042001/fallout-from-the-murder-of-real-estate-agent-beverly-carter/?#sp=show-clips
6. Ibid.
7. Lane, "Real Estate Agent Narrowly Escapes Kidnapping by Registered Sex Offender."

Chapter 3

1. Mark Boyle, "Woman Punched, Robbed at Valero Gas Station in Montrose," www.click2houston.com, June 3, 2015, http://www.click2houston.com/news/woman-punched-robbed-at-valero-gas-station-in-montrose/33385162

2. "Police Seek Gas Station Kidnapping Suspects," www.wsbtv.com, Sept. 13, 2013, http://www.wsbtv.com/news/news/local/atlanta-police-release-video-carjacking-and-kidnap/nZwQq/#__federated=1

3. Monica Garske, "Man Tried to Kidnap Woman at Gas Station: Police," www.nbcsandiego.com, Jul. 24, 2013, http://www.nbcsandiego.com/news/local/Attempted-Kidnapping-Suspect-Thomas-Paciornik-Arrested-Chula-Vista-216851561.html

4. Ibid.

Chapter 4

1. According to the Federal Highway Administration, the total number of licensed drivers is 214,092,472, https://www.fhwa.dot.gov/policyinformation/statistics/2014/dl1c.cfm

2. Marc Weber Tobias, "How Taxi Companies Rip Off Their Drivers," forbes.com, Nov. 18, 2011, http://www.forbes.com/sites/marcwebertobias/2011/11/18/how-taxi-companies-rip-off-their-drivers/

3. Derrick Parker with Matt Diehl, *Notorious C.O.P.: The Inside Story of the Tupac, Biggie, and Jam Master Jay Investigations from the NYPD's First "Hip-Hop" Cop* (New York: St. Martin's Griffin, 2006), 61

4. Manitoba Taxicab Board Report & Recommendations, November 1991, Taxicab Safety Shield, http://www.taxi-l.org/shields.htm#task

5. New York City Taxi and Limousine Commission Rule Book, chapter 67, http://www.nyc.gov/html/tlc/downloads/pdf/rule_book_current_chapter_67.pdf

6. Ibid.

7. "Taxi Partitions May Be Set for a Makeover," www.yellowcabnyctaxi.com, Aug. 5, 2009, http://www.yellowcabnyctaxi.com/nyc-taxi/taxi-partitions-set-makeover

Chapter 5

1. "Woman Robbed at Red Box Machine," KETV NewsWatch 7. July 20, 2012, http://news.yahoo.com/video/woman-robbed-red-box-machine-232545694.html;_ylt=A0LEVxKhVPBVzScAYWhXNyoA;_ylu=X3oDMTEydGZvZHRtBGNvbG8DYmYxBHBvcwMxBHZ0aWQDQjA5MzRfMQRzZWWMDc2M-

2. Ibid.

3. Bristow Marchant, Surveillance Video Released in Attempted Robbery at Rock Hill ATM," heraldonline.com, Sept. 9, 2015, http://www.heraldonline.com/news/local/crime/article34450338.html

Chapter 7

1. "NRA Gun Safety Rules," http://training.nra.org/nra-gun-safety-rules.aspx
2. Michael D. Janich, "Jim Cirillo: Modern-Day Gunfighter The Inside Story," http://www.staysafemedia.com/jim-cirillo-gunfighter

Chapter 8

1. Associated Press, "Police Say Gun Left Behind in SC Wal-Mart Bathroom," July 14, 2014, http://www.wistv.com/story/26017041/police-say-gun-left-behind-in-sc-wal-mart-bathroom
2. "Woman Left Gun in Red Robin Bathroom: Cops," nbcconnecticut.com, Mar. 3, 2014, http://www.nbcconnecticut.com/news/local/Woman-Left-Gun-in-Red-Robin-Bathroom-Cops-248231591.html
3. Hannah Hess, "Do Capital Police Problems Go Beyond the Bathroom?," rollcall.com, May 1, 2015, http://blogs.rollcall.com/hill-blotter/capitol-building-bathrooms-guns-left-behind/

Chapter 9

1. National Highway Traffic Safety Administration report (NHTSA DOT HS 809 707), http://www.nhtsa.gov/people/injury/research/AggDrivingEnf/pages/Introduction.html
2. Washington State Patrol, "Vehicle & Driver – Road Rage & Aggressive Driving," http://www.wsp.wa.gov/traveler/roadrage.htm
3. National Highway Traffic Safety Administration definition cited in Washington State Patrol.
4. Ibid.
5. Ibid.
6. http://www.merriam-webster.com/dictionary/continuum
7. Expedia's 2014 Road Rage Report by Northstar, https://viewfinder.expedia.com/news/2014-road-rage-report
8. Ibid.
9. Louis Mizell, "Aggressive Driving,"*Aggressive Driving: Three Studies,*Prepared for AAA Foundation for Traffic Safety, March 1997, https://www.aaafoundation.org/sites/default/files/agdr3study.pdf

Chapter 12

1. "The Investigation So Far," *The New York Times,* Dec. 4, 2015, http://www.nytimes.com/live/san-bernardino-shooting/the-investigation-so-far

ACKNOWLEDGMENTS

Whenever you write a book, a term paper, thesis, or shopping list, there are always other people that contribute to its content. Sometimes it's the direct result of research or merely inspiration by way of something you saw someone do that imprinted on your consciousness.

I'd like to thank Lance and Karina Loken and the Loken Group. The Loken Group changes lives. I'd like to thank Mike Weaver at Texas Armoring Corporation. TAC is one of, if not, America's premier suppliers of armored vehicles and it is a privilege to share the fascinating work they do. I'd like to thank Mike Barham at Galco Gunleather and Matt Rice for Smith and Wesson at Blue Heron Communications.

I'd like to thank David Burton, Brian Hoffner, Jay Woolley, JD Babineaux, and Joe Woolley at F.O.R.T. Texas for their insights and support. Thank you, Laser Max, for making it easy to illustrate the complex and thank you, Deb Williams, for Springfield Armory. I'd also like to thank James Burchfield, Elliott Rafter, Coach, and Jericho Gallego at American Shooting Centers.

You can't really study shooting without quality ammunition. I'd like to thank Black Hills Ammunition for their support and Vanquest for their products of innovation. With kind words spoken and just the knowledge they are there, I'd like to thank my wife and family.

When it comes to producing photographs to illustrate what you've written, you need the right people to make it work. I could refer to them as my gang, my posse, or my crew, but they're my friends whom I value and respect. I'd like to thank Craig McBride, Michael P. N. Quintero, Matt McDaris, Tommie Bryant, and Kris Babineaux. We had fun getting the pictures done and bent a few rules, too.

Finally, I'd like to thank Skyhorse for giving me all the room I needed to make this book happen and for assigning a master editor with whom I am not just on the same page but on the next page as well.

ABOUT THE AUTHOR

Roger Eckstine is one of the most prolific writers of in-depth tests and evaluations of firearms to emerge over the past twenty years. Author of the critically acclaimed *Shooter's Bible Guide to Home Defense* and the *Shooter's Bible Guide to Knives*, Eckstine brings his extraordinary eye for detail to the challenges of personal security in an increasingly complex and hostile world. A regular contributor to *KNIFE Magazine* and *Gun Tests*, his work has also appeared in *American COP* Magazine and *Predator Extreme*.

Barfield Photography